Parenting in the Pandemic

The Collision of School, Work, and Life at Home

A Collection of Essays

A Volume in Work-Life Balance

Series Editors

Joanne M. Marshall
Iowa State University

Jeffrey S. Brooks
RMIT University

Bonnie Fusarelli
North Carolina State University

Catherine A. Lugg
Rutgers University

Latish C. Reed
University of Wisconsin Milwaukee

George Theoharis
Syracuse University

Work-Life Balance

Joanne M. Marshall, Jeffrey S. Brooks, Bonnie Fusarelli,
Catherine A. Lugg, Latish C. Reed, and George Theoharis, Series Editors

Parenting in the Pandemic

The Collision of School, Work, and Life at Home

A Collection of Essays

Edited by

Rebecca Lowenhaupt
Boston College

George Theoharis
Syracuse University

INFORMATION AGE PUBLISHING, INC.
Charlotte, NC • www.infoagepub.com

Library of Congress Cataloging-in-Publication Data

CIP record for this book is available from the Library of Congress
http://www.loc.gov

ISBNs: 978-1-64802-520-4 (Paperback)

978-1-64802-521-1 (Hardcover)

978-1-64802-522-8 (ebook)

Printed in the United States of America

CONTENTS

**SECTION II: *"GOT TO GO THROUGH IT!"*:
SCHOOLING AT HOME**

SECTION III: *"WE ARE HERE FOR THE STORM"*:
SEEKING BALANCE IN THE MIDST OF CRISIS

INTRODUCTION

DOCUMENTING OUR COLLECTIVE EXPERIENCES

An Introduction to the Book

"Every moment we make a decision to write we are subjugating time. In essence we are forcing time to stop and remember us. Writing against time means we refuse to let time erase us. To write our stories down is to become timeless."

—Elisabet Velasquez

We are in the midst of a historic and tragic time in the United States that has unfolded over the last year with the COVID-19 pandemic and ongoing social upheaval in the fight for racial justice. Even as we recognize the monumental events unfolding around us, we are preoccupied with daily life. As parents, we are called to create routine and stability for our children and ourselves. As university professors, our professional obligations have continued somewhat uninterrupted. Albeit in different forms, our classes continue, deadlines remain, and we are expected to stay connected and productive despite the weight and disruptions of this time. As educators, we find ourselves in new roles as our children undergo schooling at home.

Parenting in the Pandemic: The Collision of School, Work, and Life at Home, pp. ix–xiii
Copyright © 2021 by Information Age Publishing

Some of us are teaching our own children as we once taught students in our classrooms. Others observe online school going awry. We grapple with the strange paradox that while we focus on the mundane tasks of laundry, cleaning, and preparing food, we know we are surrounded by catastrophe. Through it all, maintaining a semblance of routine falls on our shoulders as parents, partners, and professors.

In this collection of personal essays, we have come together as a community of education professors to share our experiences and reflect on the collective challenges we've faced and insights we have gathered along the way. At times, the responsibilities and weight of this time overwhelm us. But "we refuse to let time erase us," as Elisabet Velasquez puts it. With the pandemic ongoing, we hope this project will serve as an anchor to hold and comfort us in the midst of this storm.

THE PROJECT

At the start of the pandemic, we watched the educational institutions we have devoted our careers to serving transform overnight from brick-and-mortar buildings at the heart of our communities into virtual and mostly dysfunctional spaces where teachers, administrators, families, and students were rewriting school. At the same time, our family life was turned upside down as school moved home and we found ourselves in new roles as parent educators. Colliding with our expertise in education was the reality of schooling our own children in our homes during a global pandemic. The pressure and realities of the COVID-19 pandemic have placed a new set of demands on parents as school moved to online, virtual and hybrid models of learning. Families work to balance professional responsibilities with parenting and supporting their children's education.

We came to this project with the belief that education faculty, people who have deep experience and expertise in the teaching, leading, and learning of young people, have a particular vantage point on this historic moment. There are many universal and challenging aspects of pandemic parenting that these essays address and which resonate regardless of career. However, we find that our experiences as education professors with both practical, lived experience working in schools and scholarly expertise about schooling give us a different perspective on this moment and particular understandings of schooling at home. We are accustomed to wearing multiple hats as parents, educators, and scholars of education. In the pandemic, these varied identities, and the blurring of space between home and work come into conflict at multiple points and in new ways. This book explores the dilemmas that arise as we make these tensions visible through our stories.

All of us authors are academics and therefore writers in some form or other. We are accustomed to writing others' lives but writing our own is something entirely new and different for most of us. As editors, Becca and George invited our colleagues, friends, and friends of friends to submit a short personal essay that captures their experience parenting in the pandemic. We asked them to ground their essay in the daily events of their lives, telling a few specific stories that illustrate the complexities of moving through the multiple roles of being education professors and parents of school-aged children during this pandemic. We requested that they try to use these anecdotes to highlight the implications and insights they've come to during this time. Our request emphasized our hope that, despite the challenging circumstances, authors would avoid preaching or judging themselves or others in their lives. Many of us have confronted moments of despair. Yet numerous of these authors share positive lessons and deep joy, even while honoring the difficulties of this time. We also let authors know that we understand that this form of writing relies on a certain amount of authenticity, vulnerability, and courage to put our stories out into the world. As you will see, authors honored our request and rose to the challenge. On the pages that follow, we gain a window into the personal and profound. We learn from their experiences and hard-earned insights in these stories that bring to life the new reality the pandemic has brought.

OUR STORIES

In these stories, we get to know one another in new ways and share in the loss and learning of this time. On these pages, we air our insights and grievances, our small triumphs, and frequent tears through stories of our chaotic and reimagined lives in the pandemic. As education experts, we bring a particular perspective to this moment of upheaval, as we find ourselves confronting practical (and impractical) aspects of long held theories about what school could be, seeing up close and personally the pedagogy our children endure online, watching education policy go awry in our own living rooms (and kitchens and bathrooms), making high-stakes decisions about our children's (and other children's) access to opportunity, and trying to maintain our careers at the same time. In this collision of personal and professional identities, we find ourselves reflecting on fundamental questions about the purpose and design of schooling, the value of our work as education professors, and the precious relationships we hope to maintain with our children through this difficult time.

We have organized the book into three main sections. The first section is comprised of essays at the intersection of identity and justice, as authors grapple with their own senses of self as parents and professionals, commitments to equity, and social identities in the midst of both the pandemic and racial justice movements of our time. The second section turns to the nature of schooling at home. In this section, authors explore the dynamics of online classes, negotiating learning, and ways to support our children as students unmoored from the routines and community of school. The third section focuses on our efforts to regain balance in the midst of disruption. Authors share their struggle to find a balance between work, parenting, and life, grappling with the paradoxes of time that stretches and shrinks in our pandemic lives at home.

As we pulled the book together, we also invited the authors' children whose stories are told here by the parents in their lives to share images that reflected their view of parenting in the pandemic which you'll see integrated throughout the book.

KEY THEMES

Across all three sections, authors touched on similar themes which bring us together in community during this time. Throughout, these stories reveal the inescapable smog of the pandemic that creeps into all of our experiences. For some, the virus hits closer than others in essays that reference the ill and dying loved ones, family, and neighbors. For others, it feels further off yet inescapable. The tragedy is still in the atmosphere, the air we breathe, the weight of this time.

The theme of privilege is on many of our minds as educators who work on issues of equity and social justice. We acknowledge how fortunate we are in our situations and grapple with the tension between gratitude and guilt. We feel compelled to acknowledge our privilege while still sharing the pain of this time for us, while knowing others are far less fortunate. We confront the inequality that we have spent careers fighting now laid bare and exacerbated even more by the pandemic, seeking ways to combat it even as we see how our own families benefit in this time of crisis.

Gender emerged as a theme as well. In the midst of COVID, alarming research has emerged about the unequal impact this time has had on the professional trajectories of women. During this time of isolated parenting, the role many women have played as default parents and primary caregivers has had a disproportionate impact on their professional lives compared to many men. Other empirical scholarship has demonstrated this is a reality across academia. In several instances, the essays in this book provide important counternarratives to this as men take on important, oversized parenting roles as well. Despite the wide variety of experiences, parenting dynamics, and gender roles in these essays, though, the burden on women during this time does resonate as an important feminist theme.

The pain of isolation ricochets across these pages as we share similar struggles with disconnection, loneliness, and the burden of parenting without a village. Despite this isolation, there is community in our shared experiences. A common parlance has emerged, words we don't need to define in a post-pandemic world, like quarantine, Zoom, pulse oximeter, and sourdough starter, alongside the shared humor of the chaotic juggle at home.

One common term we have heard is "Learning Loss," which seems to be a misnomer given the different forms of learning described in these essays. Our kids, along with their parents, are clearly learning so much during this time, lessons we wish we didn't have to deal with and those not typically taught in school. But we are learning, and this book is flush with that.

Taken together, these stories portray a tapestry of experiences from around the country, parents of children of all ages, different racial and ethnic backgrounds, and various parenting configurations that reveal the complexity of parenting during this time of upheaval. Despite the wide range of perspectives and unique voices that come through these stories, we are held together by a common commitment to our children, our profession, and our community through this historic, disruptive, and exhausting time.

WRITING AGAINST TIME

As we write this, we know that this is not over. We are asking ourselves to reflect on the balance of this moment without a clear end to the crisis in sight. We are writing in the midst of upheaval, not in remembrance of it. This means that for many of us, it's hard to find an ending to our essay, to know what is coming next or how we will handle the months ahead. We are documenting a time in our lives, a time in history, while it still unfolds. Uncertainty is captured throughout this book. We hope the stories shared here—filled with humility and courage—speak to those who pick up this book. While separated by space and masks, we are in this moment, this crisis together.

SECTION I

"THE FIERCE URGENCY OF NOW": PANDEMIC PARENTING, JUSTICE, AND IDENTITY

> We are now faced with the fact that tomorrow is today. We are confronted with the fierce urgency of now. In this unfolding conundrum of life and history, there "is" such a thing as being too late. This is no time for apathy or complacency. This is a time for vigorous and positive action.
>
> —Reverend Doctor Martin Luther King Jr.

Time warped during the COVID-19 pandemic. Days, weeks and months blurred together. We had more time at home with immediate family and house mates, less time with others. But in the midst of feeling that perhaps tomorrow is today or tomorrow was yesterday, parenting for many of us was grounded in the fierce urgency of now that the Reverend Dr. King called us to feel. And how could we not think of his words during this time? As the fight for racial justice intensified through the spring and summer, we felt the urgency of our time play out as the pandemic and the fight for justice laid bare the systemic inequalities facing our country.

In our daily lives, both the pandemic and crisis of racial injustice played out together across our lives and communities, forcing us parents to take vigorous action:

To confront both pandemic and racial injustice at the same time with our children.

To confront them daily.

To confront them immediately.

To confront them because we feared being too late.

In this set of essays, parents wrestled with how to move through these crises. How could they live up to their ideals? What did their identities mean in this moment? How could they protect their children? What positive actions could they take with their children? How could they frame this time and help their children make sense of it? And how, amidst the burdens of daily life, could they confront injustice even in some small way?

This first section of the book is heavy with the weight of parental urgency. As you will read in the essays that follow, parents are finding ways, big and small, to confront the moment. In the face of racial trauma, parents hold fast to their children and their children's spirits—talking, laughing, weeping, singing and leaning into the stories of ancestors. In the face of classist assumptions, parents serve ice cream. In the face of wrestling with identity, parents hold on tight to closet cleaning, baking and extra morning snuggles. These moving essays are grounded in the realities of the COVID pandemic and the struggle for racial justice, and intersect with the diverse identities these professor parents bring to this moment of urgency.

CHAPTER 1

ICE CREAM FOR BREAKFAST

Vincent Cho

"Dear Teacher with a No Food Rule, I'm sorry I served ice cream during your Zoom. We needed breakfast." I tweeted this midmorning on September 24. It's possible that the ice cream was actually second breakfast, either because the first one got rejected or because I'd served something like oatmeal, which is a hunger trap. It never tides anyone over. I do remember being in our kitchen, which is only slightly larger than the galley of my in-laws' RV. I mention this, because I recall the pressure cooker feeling of living in a tiny house, the eerily warm not-summer day that is both pleasant and commingled with ecological anxiety. Throughout the pandemic, I have been the default parent, juggling work and house stuff, plus providing tech support, personal assistant, and janitorial services for one fourth and one first grade virtual learner. This is all to say that pandemic parenting has left me feeling a little frayed.

But of course, that wasn't my gripe with the "No Food Rule." Our teachers had been pushing rules hard since before day one, with e-mail notices and daily lectures. In fact, since my kids get all their specials in a single Friday morning block of 30-minute sprints per teacher, there was even one day where everyone spent their entire mornings being lectured on the rules. It was all the same rules. No one had different ones. None of us on the audience side had the courage to say, "Uhm, we heard this

Parenting in the Pandemic: The Collision of School, Work, and Life at Home, pp. 3–6
Copyright © 2021 by Information Age Publishing

already." Rather, my reaction at the time was partly of shock. I couldn't tell how far people were going to take the whole rules thing. Looking back on my child, I used to love seeing Mr. Rogers on TV. He visited my home, and I visited his. I'm positive he'd have been ok that we were eating and sitting on the couch. He liked us, just the way we are.

By late September, however, my misgivings were intensifying. Unlike certain houses in town, our house was not a (no kidding) crenellated castle. Unlike one family we know, we do not summer at our second house on its own little island. Rather, we are known among my daughter's classmates as the "tiny house." Our unit has two bedrooms. Taller people must duck to enter the bathroom; once there, they find that the sink and toilet are actually the slightly miniaturized versions found in corner half baths. For my work spaces, I choose between a dusty, unfinished basement (where even I have to duck), or the couch (while wearing 3M earmuffs, as seen on flight decks). This is all to say that when teachers opened the year with lectures that every child needed a personal and "proper" work space ("No couches! No distractions!"), my heart began to sink. I was dumbfounded when the homework was to take photos of one's work areas (plus separate "reading nooks").

That same week, they were also doing various assignments reporting about how much "fun" summer had been. I wondered how my children rode through these fissions in reality. It hurt me, did it hurt them? I am the first in my family to go to college, and I got there by doing homework on the couch, while eating, while the TV was on. I had been raised by my mom, who had emigrated here from China. One of my earliest memories is of being strapped to her back while she cooked in a family restaurant. By the time I was school-aged, she sewed in a factory; by night she did alterations for my uncle's dry cleaners. When asked the "summer fun" question in school, I often felt left behind. It wasn't until I had my own family and began actively planning experiences for them that I got an inkling for the many possibilities. I had to give that up this year. People we distantly knew had gotten sick; two distant family members had even died. My wife was unable to work, and we had lost income. We did not have fun this pandemic. The best I could figure out were a couple of hours at the beach, just as crowds were going home for the day. It felt surreal for school to expect anything more. I knew that some of these expectations were classist and invasive. I felt it. Did others?

Although I had e-mailed some of my qualms to certain teachers, I could see it wasn't clicking. They certainly weren't reading any articles or infographics I'd attach—not when they were responding to e-mail at 10 P.M. I wasn't sure how hard to push, since I could only imagine their own personal and professional juggling acts. But then I also noticed how hard certain teachers were bearing down on the "Camera Always On Rule."

My daughter would now get snappy if one of us crossed through the living room behind her. She started wearing shoes, because her teacher told them to dress for "real school." Sometimes he did activities where they had to hold their shod feet to the camera, and she didn't want to get in trouble.

On the morning of the ice cream, I think I was hoping to test the consequences of breaking one of these rules. I had a speech that began with, "This is our house, and we're the ones who get to make the rules." But as it was, my son ate his ice cream unnoticed. Alternatively, my daughter, perhaps seeing through my ploy, decided to let hers melt. She's nobody's pawn. In replaying this fight I didn't get to pick, I also felt like there were other things I wanted to say. It wasn't just about the rules or the privacy or sanctity of our home. It wasn't just about revisiting my own personal experiences of class and difference.

Rather, I was also catching up to the realization that my daughter's teacher, in particular, was using rules to bully students for differences and circumstances outside of their control. Citing the "camera on rule," he gave students a hard time if their videos were muted. When those children finally did reveal themselves, we saw that they were in kitchens, or had other children about, or maybe just didn't want people to see their clutter. My daughter approached me with worries to me about how those kids might have felt, adding that she felt he held "grudges" against them. She noted that these were the same kids he would threaten to boot from Zoom because their first names were listed incorrectly—they were on borrowed devices and unable to change screen names. As I listened in over the next few days, I also noticed that these were the same students who didn't have an adult nearby to help with other issues, such as glitchy audio, finding a misplaced notebook, or interpreting assignment instructions. He made faces and speeches about how they should be able to figure things out on their own. It gnawed at me that it was never the White students that he hassled. After a few days, I decided to speak to our principal.

In reflecting about these experiences and about pandemic life more generally, I would like to recognize how hard it is for any of us to know which expectations to hold onto and which to let go of. Rules would seem to impose clarity, predictability, and order. The problem is that they don't always fit the situations at hand. One last story: realizing some students were not paying attention, our teacher attempted the "all eyes on me" tactic, forcing students to stare into the abyss of their cameras until everyone was on board. It didn't work. In Zoom, there was no shushing of friends, no ripple of realization and quiet. It was grueling.

To be fair, I think it is wrong to expect that when tossed into the air, we should all be able to fly. However, it is also wrong to find ourselves tossed in the air and to pretend otherwise. Some teachers have been remarkable at finding new rules and norms, new ways of doing things that still fit their values, goals, and circumstances. I have been continually amazed at how my son's teacher has found ways to make students feel academically and personally cared for. I was especially moved one morning when we found her Zooming from a frozen airfield, touring an airplane with the class. Turning toward the moment, even if it's uncomfortable or not what we're used to, invites a special sort of freedom. It is freedom to respond to what's in front of us, not to the ghosts of what ought to be.

For me, on the morning of September 24, with some things holding together and others falling apart, that meant having ice cream during class. Most of us were in pajamas. I even added sprinkles.

CHAPTER 2

FOR EVERYTHING THERE IS A SEASON

Jennie Weiner

A couple of weeks ago, just as the New England leaves burst into bright reds and yellows, and that little autumn chill fought through to remind us a new season was coming, we, my husband, Jeremiah, and 9-year-old twin boys, Manny and Rufus, completed our annual ritual of changing out our spring/summer for our fall/winter clothes. As many people who live in spaces with too small closets or too big wardrobes can tell you, this day is filled with lots of activity as the things that no longer fit (the boys for good reasons, for us, not so much) or were kept for reasons unknown (why do I need 10 black cardigans?) are folded and put in bags to be given away and the keepers are put away in various closets and drawers.

While I hate housework of all kinds, I usually find this ritual comforting and even enjoyable. The changing of seasons, the excitement of a new school year and possibilities, the opportunity to put on that sweater I loved so much or to hang back up that dress I save for conferences (it doesn't wrinkle!) and sometimes wear to enjoy an evening out with friends, makes me hopeful and happy. This year however, as I stood there with my old life strewn around my bedroom, the loss was so palpable it brought me to tears. I am no longer that woman, someone with somewhere to

Parenting in the Pandemic: The Collision of School, Work, and Life at Home, pp. 7–10
Copyright © 2021 by Information Age Publishing

go, something to dress up for. I miss my students, I miss my colleagues, but perhaps most of all I miss me, and the person, the professional—the woman—I used to be.

Since my boys were born, I have spent much of my time, and far too much of my emotional energy, trying to meet the multiple, and often competing, expectations of being a "good" mother and partner while simultaneously building my academic career. I have, over the years, pumped breast milk in an airplane toilet so I could make it to a conference to present on my dissertation while my boys were nursing, regularly left my house for work at 4:30 A.M. so I could leave the office by 3 P.M. to make it soccer games, concerts, kung fu belt ceremonies, and so forth. I have said no to conferences I wanted to attend, and yes to others that I didn't, but were a better fit with our schedule. I have done everything I could to make the impossible possible, often to mixed effects. While, of course, this frantic dancing facilitated meeting my commitments, I often felt like I was invisible. When you are constantly a blur, it is hard to see even your own outline clearly.

In recent years, as I have gotten older and moved up (tenure helps), I have felt this outline come back into a bit more focus. The boys, though still needing much, are a bit less dependent on us. My husband, always a true partner, has taken on far more than 50% of the home labor to accommodate my schedule. We also got far fewer midday calls from school, as Manny is now in a specialized program that better meets his needs. As a result, I started taking some more time for myself—exercising regularly, for example, joining a book club and making more choices about my time and what I wanted to do with it. Trips away, some for pleasure just with friends, became less anxiety provoking and fraught. All of the sudden, when I looked in the mirror, I thought I saw someone I recognized. Then COVID happened.

Since March 13, 2020 (but who's counting), I have been home with my sons, who, despite attending a school in a district with a hybrid plan have yet to step foot into a classroom since the pandemic began. In the meantime, I have been a paraprofessional, counselor, PE teacher, IT gal, and lunch lady. I have been *Mom, Mommy, Mama, Hey You*, and from Jeremiah, *My Love* or just, *Jennie*. Sometimes, when I attend a virtual defense or teach on zoom late at night, I am Dr. or Professor Weiner, but mostly I am just Jennie. Jennie, who is finding unexpected joy in small moments with my sons, seeing their resilience and independence in the face of so much change, helping them with their reading or watching them engage in building a flashlight or kick a soccer ball or just, for no reason, coming over during the day and giving me a hug. Jennie, who again wakes up at 4:45 A.M. to work before the boys' school day starts, and stays up too late, and drinks too much wine, and still misses her students, and frets over how they and their families are, and wants to help but doesn't know how. Jennie, who feels so conflicted about her school system's response as she watches our communities' most vulnerable children and families lose access to all the essential service schools provide, and our city's bar hours and restaurant seating get expanded. Jennie, who feels enraged at the failure of our federal government for dealing with this crisis and towards all those in the policy arena who have looked away as working mothers, due to lack of meaningful childcare, and unaddressed discriminatory policies around everything from maternal leave to pay equity, have dropped out of the workforce en masse. Jennie, who sometimes just feels like it is all just too much, and she is too little to make it all work.

And then I breathe, go upstairs, and open the door to my closet. I see those clothes and remember that the woman who wore them is me, that I am her. Yes, getting her back is going to be hard, and that she might be, just like those clothes going largely unused, a bit worse for wear, but she is still there, and she is waiting for me. And so, I put it on, the conference dress (with leggings and slippers), and run downstairs to serve snacks and dole out encouragement and maybe, just maybe, get a few minutes of writing done in the moments between (see Figures 2.1 & 2.2).

Figure 2.1

Mom's Always at Home 1 by Manny (age 9)

Figure 2.2

Mom's Always at Home 2 by Rufus (age 9)

CHAPTER 3

PRIVILEGING LOVE DURING A DOUBLE PANDEMIC

Gretchen Givens Generett

I was not born into a family that had financial privilege. I was, however, born into a family that knew how to pour love into you. They privileged love. Today, I have the honor of parenting two Black children, William a 19-year-old first year student at Morehouse College, and Gabrielle a 13-year-old middle school student. They are wonderful children that have grown into smart, insightful, and thoughtful young people. This pandemic has been a challenge for them and for their father and I, and yet as I sit to write this essay, I am overwhelmed by the gratitude that I feel for them, that my family is healthy, and that our needs are being met. While our lives are drastically different since the virus started, I am ever more aware of our financial and educational privileges and of how their childhood is different from mine. Working from home is stressful, but unlike friends who have little children, my kids are old enough to be self-sufficient and academically, have transitioned well to online learning. They miss their normal social interactions (as we all do) and they are tethered to their electronics in ways that we would not have allowed prior to the stay-at-home orders, but we are managing.

Parenting in the Pandemic: The Collision of School, Work, and Life at Home, pp. 11–13

This feeling of gratitude has evolved for me. Who could have imagined that our lives would be like this months ago when this pandemic started? Friday, March 13, 2020 was my last day on campus for the 2020 Spring semester. As we sat in the conference room listening to the dissertation defense that had been scheduled months before, I was inundated with text messages. The first came from, William, who was in his senior year in high school. "We are being told that we might not come back to school." The next text came from Gabrielle, "Did you hear that we might be out of school for a while?" The next message was from a colleague, "The University is going fully online on Monday. Should we move our Saturday classes online too?" The quick decisions that had to be made without knowing what this virus really meant for any of us, made me anxious. It was (is) surreal.

As the spring semester began to wind down, I realized that there would be no senior year celebration for William and that I would most likely not see my Mother in Virginia for months. My anxiety turned to sadness and rage as I watched the video of Ahmaud Arbery being hunted down by racists. Stuck in the house with work as our only distraction, my husband, children, and I could not turn away or turn off the constant trauma of watching another Black man killed because of the color of his skin. Then there was Amy Copper in Central Park who called the cops on a Black man who was bird watching and we watched and cried together as the life left George Floyd's body while Derek Chauvin, a white police officer, knelt on his neck for nearly 9 minutes. We sat in silence as we witnessed cities burn and protestors shout, "Say her name" in honor of Breonna Taylor who was shot to death by law enforcement serving a no-knock warrant to the wrong address. We deliberated as a family whether or not it was safe enough to participate in the protests in our city and if we did, how it would impact our health given COVID-19 and the preexisting medical conditions in our family.

It doesn't interest me to know where you live or how much money you have. I want to know if you can get up, after the night of grief and despair, weary and bruised to the bone, and do what needs to be done to feed the children.

—*The Invitation by Oriah*

The first time I read this excerpt of the poem, *The Invitation* (Dreamer, 1999), I was a new mother, and it was early in my academic career. It reminded me of my own mother, grandmothers, and great-grandmothers. I wondered what grief they bore as they fed their own children and other people's children?

Parenting during a double pandemic, the coronavirus and systemic racism, has me thinking a lot about the mothers who helped to rear me and the lessons they modeled. Parenting Black children in the U.S. is hard. Parenting Black children during a time where you have to sit and be still with the toxic stress of racism without distractions or the coping strategies and your support systems, is harder. My household has always been aware of, impacted by, and busy fighting racism. Systemic racism is the pandemic that built this country and the one that shaped my life and the lives of my ancestors. Stories passed down to me of how my ancestors navigated the racism pandemic in the U.S. are instructive every day, but especially during times of crisis. These stories are filled with courage, resilience, hard work, and perseverance. They are also filled with disappointments, struggles, and loss. In spite of racism and despite life's ups and downs, I was privileged by the love that I felt and witnessed, by the models of giving and sharing, of making room for one more. Upon reflection, the challenges, anxiety, and worry that I experience as a mother of Black children is perhaps the one true similarity that my life has with the women in my family who came before me. Having their lives as examples, I know that I (my family) will be alright during and after this pandemic. Why? Because I acknowledge and understand the pervasiveness and debilitating impact of racism prior to the coronavirus. The fact that we are all "caught in an inescapable network of mutuality, tied in a single garment of destiny" (King, 1963, p. 77) is not a new revelation to me. For historically oppressed people, community and collectivity are not optional ways of being in the world. Sadly, I am not surprised by Americans who understand themselves as having access to rights, autonomy, and independence to forgo interrelatedness for false narratives of individualism. As we have seen, we cannot get rid of the coronavirus without depending on our neighbors to wear a mask and we cannot rid the world of racism and injustices without ensuring that the human rights and privileges espoused by this country are granted to everyone.

Currently, I find myself telling my children what the Mothers in my family told me. Be who we know you are and not who they say or think you are. Model love for people who have not had love modeled for them. When my children say that I am being idealistic or old-fashioned, I tell them that we are where we are because our ancestors understood this. They lived lives that made our lives possible. After nights of grief and despair, weary and bruised to the bone, they did what was needed to be done to feed the children. I am so very grateful for the mothers in my life who privileged love.

REFERENCES

Dreamer, O. M. (1999). *The invitation*. HarperCollins.
King, M. L., Jr. (1963). *Why we can't wait*. Penguin.

CHAPTER 4

DEAR ISABELLA

Dalia Rodriguez

Dear Isabella,

It wasn't the dailiness of juggling a work schedule with homeschooling, the online school-work you were assigned in the spring that was a problem during the pandemic. Nor was it keeping up with the endless dirty dishes, laundry, and the impossibility of being productive with scholarship and teaching. But rather, it was the witnessing of the pain and trauma that you experienced as a result of the pandemic and the continuous killing of Black lives that affected you so.

It was late and you were having trouble falling asleep, tossing, and turning, as you got twisted up in the blanket. I finally asked, "Are you ok?" You have always had trouble sleeping. Looking up at me, you responded, "Mom … I don't wanna die … I don't want you to die," as you began sobbing into your pillow. How do I assure you that I will not die? How do I look at you and tell you that, if I can't guarantee it myself? How can I lie to you when I know I'm immunocompromised and my anxiety shot through the roof at the beginning of the pandemic? All I could do was hold you and try to reassure you "We are going to be ok … we're gonna get through this," as we held each other and eventually fell asleep.

Parenting in the Pandemic: The Collision of School, Work, and Life at Home, pp. 15–17
Copyright © 2021 by Information Age Publishing

Every afternoon we would sit watching Lester Holt on the evening news. We stared at the TV with bodies being carried into large white semi-trucks, and endless news reports of NYC police shooting through crowds of peaceful Black Lives Matter protests. Night after night, we watched, as police across the country continued killing Black men across the country. The night we saw George Floyd's wife being interviewed, with their daughter sitting right next to her, you started crying, "Mom! I'm scared! What if the police kill my dad?" At 8 years old, you were scared for your father's life, understandably so … this is the reality of being young and Black in America.

It was summer, and the days had been hot and humid. Despite the humidity, we decided to go on a bike ride to escape our home. We had been quarantining for three months and going outside was our only reprieve from being home all day. As we rode through yet another neighborhood, you put your brakes on, so I slowed down, finally stopping. One day, you looked at me and asked, "What if the police kill ME? Cuz they kill Black girls too, not just Black men! They do! I saw it on the news mom!" as if you were trying to convince me of what I already knew to be true. Your fear continued to build as we watched Breonna Taylor's story unfold.

We began having conversations about the Black Lives Matter protests prompted by the deaths of George Floyd as well as Breonna Taylor. We had always talked about social justice issues, but given the social and political climate, we spent our summer days talking intensely about race relations and what it means to be Black in America.

No amount of books, training, late nights writing, years of reading, could have prepared me for this moment. I had seen you so sad for months—not being able to see your friends, witnessing state violence against Blacks on TV and the endless pandemic, and I myself struggling with depression, we needed nature to help in our healing. I packed some sandwiches, threw some iced water bottles along with some of those Polar Ice juices we both had been enjoying that summer when we'd stop by the local pharmacy for a break from our long bike rides. You helped Mom carry the beach chairs, as best as you could, as one chair slipped of your shoulder, taking frequent breaks, setting them down, as we trudged along the beach. We got out into the water … I felt out of it that day, the day was hazy, but the sun was shining bright, and being in the water felt freeing. As you did your flips in the water, you suddenly popped your head up and said, "I wonder what it would be like to die?" Those words made my world stand still.

Throughout the pandemic, I witnessed how you became depressed. I can still see the sadness in your eyes, when I would ask, "What's wrong?" Laying down on your bed, looking away from me, as the tears rolled down on your pillow. It hurt to know that I could not keep you from feeling that pain. I could not protect you. I stayed up till 6 A.M. scouring the internet for therapists to call first thing on Monday morning. I found a national organization and I called every single therapist listed. No luck. Morning news broadcasters and talk show hosts talked about the need for mental health during the pandemic. But what they often failed to mention was that nationally, there is simply a shortage of therapists—even less so if you are seeking a therapist of color.

The pandemic has meant taking the time to just BE with each other, to really listen. Despite the lack of a therapist, you slowly tamed those fears. I know that becoming friends with those you connect with on your game apps helped tremendously. Our frequent trips to the park and spending as much time outside in nature has helped us both. I remember you saying, "I feel sorta normal" as you swung on the tire swing, looking up at the sky. Though, the other part of it was your own strength. Like the time I heard you yelling from the living room "You are a racist! I'm reporting you!" As I ran from the kitchen, I found you playing on your game app, where apparently someone had claimed that all Blacks and Mexicans should die.

Those of us who nurture the lives of children of color who are hated, despised, ignored, and/or silenced, mothering is the most revolutionary work we can do. And it is in this spirit that I try to mother you. At the center of mothering ourselves and each other is the spirit of love. I show you as much love as I possibly can. Radical mothering means raising you to look at yourself honestly, and encouraging you to continuously question yourself, your own actions, and holding yourself accountable to other people of color. It also means raising a daughter that is strong in her opinion and willing to take chances and stand up to a white supremacist and patriarchal system when you are a witness to and/or experience injustices. But I also want you to feel … to feel deeply as Lorde puts it, to not deny the fear, anger, doubts, and all of the feelings we feel as girls and women of color due to systems of oppression. As Lorde says, "to feel fear, but not be overwhelmed by it."

With much love,

Mom

CHAPTER 5

PANDEMIC HOMESCHOOLING AND DECISIONS MADE OF CARE AND FEAR

Susan W. Woolley

The school bus barrels down the hill, autumn leaves kicked up as it speeds by, delivering children to the K–12 public school by 7:47. I hear one of my twins whisper, "Mommy! Snuggle!" before he climbs into bed with me to start off his day with a cuddle. I slowly work on opening my eyes, rubbing the sleep from the corners, to the new reality that has emerged around me in 2020. I wake up to this new reality and new routines where things do not look the same. Sleeping in past 6 A.M. as well as not having to rush my children onto that school bus are welcome changes to our lives, especially since my insomnia has gone off the rails during the pandemic and many of my work hours have shifted to after my kids go to bed.

The mornings are punctuated by the same routines and necessary labor of getting the day going, and as such, do not look all that different than the before-times, except now everything home and work are interwoven together. I make sure morning chores like walking the dog, taking out the garbage and recycling, starting the laundry, straightening up and making the beds as well as the tasks of feeding the children breakfast, wrangling

Parenting in the Pandemic: The Collision of School, Work, and Life at Home, pp. 19–23
Copyright © 2021 by Information Age Publishing
All rights of reproduction in any form reserved.

them toward getting dressed, doing the dishes, and cleaning up are taken care of before heading downstairs to work.

It is 9:49 and I am standing at my desk, opening the document, and beginning to write, hoping for just 15, maybe 20 wonderful minutes of freewriting this morning, as the patter of four feet running across the floor above me in my basement office are followed by four more feet of a zooming puppy. The twins chase each other down the hallway, a brief break in their studies, and I wonder how they would handle schooling this year, sitting in a classroom with a mandate to not move from their seats for safety protocol.

My wife begins their homeschool day with either yoga or music class to get their bodies awake before diving into literacy and handwriting work. In our kitchen, she teaches our 5-year-old how to read and write. Her many years of experience as a middle-school science teacher ground her in her constructivist and child-centered pedagogy and curriculum development. Although the subjects of literacy and numeracy—their foundations, their emergent forms, their basic practices—have not been the content of her teaching in the past, her craft and trade as an educator make the transition to homeschooling as seamless as possible.

Meanwhile I try to work in an office downstairs, holding space for and sometimes crying with students in our office hours sessions, advising, grading, reading, prepping for class, teaching classes on zoom, taking care of bureaucratic paperwork as a program director, attending administration meetings and committee meetings, writing letters of recommendation, and trying to write and maintain some kind of scholarly trajectory.

The decision to homeschool our 5-year-old twins during a global pandemic rather than send them to kindergarten in the local public school was not an easy choice for our family. We understood the implications of pulling two students out of the local school in terms of government money divested away from public education by our move. As a scholar and product of public education with deep commitments to public education, that move was not made without considerable weight on my conscious. As a teacher educator who works closely with preservice and in-service teachers in the community, the move was also not one made out of any kind of criticism of our local district's response, but rather a desire to alleviate some of the pressure of educating all of the community's children in this time.

My wife and I, as educators, understood what our kids as active energetic curious 5-year-olds need in terms of development and learning, and we knew that we could provide that for them at home in this unprecedented moment. By taking our kids out of the school, we could reduce the numbers and make more space available for children of families with essential workers or less flexibility and privilege than us. My family has resources in space, flexibility in my schedule, and two parents with decades of experience teaching K–12 and developing curriculum. We knew we could provide for them an education in basic literacy and numeracy, handwriting, and the arts and sciences while finding opportunities for them to socialize and play with others so that they may practice negotiating, sharing, taking turns, listening, empathizing, and taking care of their friends, and remain connected while they are being homeschooled. We knew we could provide for them a learning environment in which inquiry and exploration through their senses were at the heart of what they are doing, rather than mediated by a screen. We also felt we owed it to the local teachers to take on managing just ourselves, our curriculum, and our execution of that rather than get stressed out trying to implement the school teacher's lesson plans and remote learning at home. That is, in this moment we would rather take responsibility for our children's education than place that burden on teachers who are already being asked to do too much for our society in these times.

Admittedly, I had been waiting for years for my children to enter kindergarten! In fact, long before they were conceived the question of which district to move into always factored into play, the question of how we would organize our family travel around the academic calendar—the anticipation of schooling, even before we had kids, structured our considerations. I had been waiting for years for this rite of passage of starting a child's journey through K–12 schooling and beyond, but also the rite of passage for me. I was looking forward to the stability that compulsory public K–12 schooling affords working parents and caregivers. I was looking forward to the public childcare that goes along with all the teaching and love that teachers provide and some of the relief of more regular childcare in the form of a school's daily schedule and after-school programming. That is, selfishly, somewhere in my heart I had hoped to resume a more normal workday schedule. But, really the greatest loss was that I had been waiting for years for my children to also learn from Ms. Pleasant* (a pseudonym), the local kindergarten teacher I had been working and cooperating with for years. Long before my children were born, I had begun placing my own undergraduate and graduate pre-service teachers in Ms. Pleasant's classroom to observe her teaching, to learn from her, and to help her in class. I had been excited for the day my kids would get to join her classroom, which I knew was populated by all kinds of literacy and music, movement, and cooperative work amongst the students. The loss of my children getting to be Ms. Pleasant's students, to be in the classroom among their peers, to start their K–12 educational trajectory like "normal" feels like another among many things taken by the pandemic.

It is 1:39 and I run to the hardware store and grocery store in between class and a meeting to attend to my family's and home's needs. I was the shopper for the family for a while at the beginning of the pandemic because the rise of anti-Asian violence and hate made my wife wary of putting herself in particular spaces in our white rural community in antici- pation of racial microaggressions or more hateful acts. The decision to do homeschool kindergarten during a pandemic has allowed us to redirect our time and energy toward educating our children, while serving as a risk management strategy. Homeschooling allows us to mitigate some of the risks of contracting and spreading the virus, but even more so, to mitigate the risks of the toil that everyday anxiety can wreak. I must acknowledge that our decision, while borne and possible because of our class privilege, was one made of fear.

A smaller fear of our kids starting off on their schooling journey at a time when schooling does not look the same;

Fears of our kids coming to dislike school early in their careers because they cannot do some of the things they would normally do or would like to do, like share toys and play with friends, eat together at lunch, and sing together;

Bigger fears of disease and death as a family with underlying medical con- ditions defined by the Centers for Disease Control and Prevention that put one at increased risk of severe illness from the virus that causes COVID-19 and as a family that has experienced loss of life due to COVID-19;

Fears of practices by anti-masking members of our communities and their kids and related fears of community spread;

But probably the biggest fear was that of the anxiety produced in anticipa- tion of everyday racism. As a mixed-race queer family living in a con- servative rural county where folks think the pandemic is a hoax, actively anti-mask, are armed and ready for a race war, and fly the Confederate flag approximately 250 miles north of the Mason-Dixon line, we have never felt safe, but these feelings have been exacerbated by the pandemic. Since the pandemic began, my wife who is Chinese-American and has always felt highly visible and vulnerable as a woman of color in a white rural land- scape has felt even more visible and vulnerable as anti-Asian hate crimes have increased while politicians politicize a deadly virus with racist rhetoric of the "Chinese virus" and "Kung flu."

So, for us, homeschooling has offered everyone more space in the vec- tors of six feet, more space in our lives and schedules to snuggle in the morning and weave together home, schooling, and work. Homeschooling has also provided us more space to breathe in the vectors of everyday rac- ism in a White supremacist society. Slowing down the rhythms of our lives, trying to center care as we attend to our fears and the anxiety that fear produces, we are finding a new home/school/work balance that makes space for the unexpected and routine.

CHAPTER 6

PRIVILEGE DOESN'T MEAN YOU DIDN'T WORK HARD

George Theoharis

Ferguson (2014), a South African feminist, defines privilege with 5 components. "1) Privilege is the other side of oppression. 2) We need to understand privilege in the context of power systems. 3) Privilege and oppression affect each other but do not negate each other. 4) Privilege describes what everyone should experience." The fifth, being "privileged doesn't mean you didn't work hard." The COVID pandemic has forced me to work extremely *hard* across multiple areas of my life; and my PRIVILEGE is right there, every step of the way.

Teaching: Now that our education world is Zoom-centric, it takes a lot to have to match my shirt and tie with my pajama pants. Perhaps more pressing, how do I change my in-person activity-oriented 3-hour classes to account for Zoom fatigue, and the realities and limitations of online interaction? It sure takes a lot of hard work redoing all my classes to adjust to this new environment.

Planning for teacher education programs: I don't think it is too much to ask that my undergrad student teachers wear shirts to Zoom class (I'm looking at you fellas). More importantly, how do we prepare future teachers if schools (understandably) do not want student teachers because of the

Parenting in the Pandemic: The Collision of School, Work, and Life at Home, pp. 25–29
Copyright © 2021 by Information Age Publishing
25

realities of COVID? It sure takes a lot of hard work figuring out how to do teacher education with little interaction in schools.

Running a household: It's 11:00 P.M., where can I find toilet paper? As a divorced Dad, it sure takes a lot of hard work solo running a household in the best of times, and now there are so many more constraints.

Caring for my aging parents who live in my house: With 2 kids and 2 parents living in my house, I now have 4 people who do not want to listen to me. (My kids are much better listeners than my parents, FYI.). My mother who found happiness in lots of little and big things was a fierce activist; she had dementia, lung cancer, COPD, multiple strokes and seizures, diabetes, etc. She got pneumonia during the pandemic and her O^2 level was 78. Every year we end up in the hospital, but how can I avoid taking her to the hospital during COVID? We avoided the hospital for 2 illnesses, including that pneumonia. But her third illness (not COVID) during the pandemic was her end, and necessitated going to the hospital. She passed away painlessly and relatively quickly, but alone. It sure takes a lot of hard work caring for my parents who moved in because they could not care for themselves. Most days it feels like another full-time job.

Being part of a 2-household love relationship: When we stream the *Marvelous Mrs. Maisel* over Zoom using screen sharing, we can still pause to talk about Mrs. Maisel's fabulous orange flower dress. The more pressing issue is, since we don't live in the same house, our shelter-in-place bubble means we are apart. As the COVID rates have surged, we haven't been in the same physical space in over 2 months, I wonder when we will hold hands again? It sure takes a lot of hard emotional work to be apart from the one you love.

These things are hard. Many days I am exhausted. Many days I sit in the quiet when no one else is awake and think, even though this is hard...

> *...I have the luxury of a job where I can work from home in the comfort of my PJ pants.*
>
> *...I have a job that provides solid healthcare benefits.*
>
> *...My job provides a comfortable financial reality.*
>
> *...My work is rewarding and I get to contribute to something bigger than myself.*
>
> *...I don't have to worry about racial profiling or police/vigilante violence directed at my kids or me.*
>
> *...I have close family, colleagues and a partner who support and love me very much.*

Even as I work hard, there are so many things I don't have to worry about. I see my PRIVILEGE every day. But the thing I think about the most is the PRIVILEGE I have in parenting.

I am blessed to get to parent two teenagers—Sam, 18, and Ella, 16. They are kind, thoughtful, funny and perceptive adolescents … adolescents tho, they are, complete with needing 7 reminders to mow the lawn, weeks of nudging that these things called "closets" and "dressers" might be better places to keep clean clothes than the wall-to-wall laundry-on-the-floor aesthetic; plenty of sass, selective listening and eye rolls. (I am clearly biased about them.) Anyone who parents adolescents knows it is hard work.

When the pandemic began the move to distance learning meant school became less taxing and less time consuming for my two teenagers. Sam was a senior in high school, Ella, a sophomore. School comes easy for them, they are responsible and self-directed learners, and they excel in traditional learning. I know so many other parents are stretched to breaking having to support, supervise, teach and cajole their children while balancing their home/work life. Despite the horror of the unfolding COVID spread, each day I feel the PRIVILEGE of the ease of remote learning for my children. Getting to savor and appreciate my kids in this new way is a beautiful experience for me during all of this mess.

The week my kids' high school shut down for COVID was supposed to be the annual high school musical. Both Ella and Sam had spent months of hard work preparing for *Les Misérables*. Sam had a leading role as Thenardier—the master of house; Ella was running the sound board and had worked for months building the elaborate set. The last day of school before the shutdown should have been the weekend of the show but the musical got canceled. Sadness and anger swept across the over 100+ students in the cast and crew.

No spring music department trip, no awards nights, no graduation, no prom, no senior ball, no end of the year concerts. No outings or hanging out with friends. No yearbook day. No senior improv club show. Ella turned 16 and could not get her driver's permit right away because the DMV was closed. Many small losses. Some of them were hard to take. Despite the irritation and real sadness, none of these things were traumatic. Pandemic parenting means supporting Ella and Sam to sit with their sadness and disappointment and to also see and articulate the PRIVILEGE we are experiencing, not the big disruption, loss, trauma, and danger so many families face. It is a PRIVILEGE to have just an accumulation of small losses.

With the move to distance learning for them and with me working remotely, we are at home together. The schooling reality for my kids is that school now is less time consuming, and there are no other activities, so we have a bounty of time to be together. With our ethnic commitment to food, more time with my kids means more time for cooking and baking. Like many others, we make homemade carbs every week—focaccia, biscuits, tortillas, pita, gnocchi. And, on Thursday, we bake! We make cookies and bars, cake-pops, and croissants. Thursday nights we drive around blasting the week's Spotify playlist, and deliver little boxes of treats to friends, neighbors, colleagues, and my kids' teachers. (The teachers seemed to appreciate it the most.) Baking for dozens and dozens of people each week is hard work, but what a PRIVILEGE to be able to have this time and experience with my kids.

I would not have imagined getting to spend so much time with Sam his final spring of high school and what should be the start of college. Sam was supposed to be off to college this fall; but his college decided 1st year students would begin in January, so he was home. This was hard and disappointing for him as all his friends went off to college. He had an online internship, took one online college class, and supports 5 families with elementary and middle school students with their remote learning. He was very busy and worked hard as he scooted from remote learning support to his own class to internship work. But I got to be with him to support his navigating mature issues around safety and responsibility to others in terms of public health. This time with him was a real gift of PRIVILEGE.

I see that my work takes increasing time and energy. I have days of 5, 6, 7 hours of Zoom teaching and meetings. I have to adapt all my teaching to online. My body has new aches and pains from all the ZOOMing and all the sitting. Since work and home are now completely blurred, sometimes it feels like I am expected to always be working. E-mail floods in, students call and text, meetings get scheduled for all hours. This takes a lot of hard work. Yet, every day I recognize I am sitting in tremendous privilege as a white male full professor. I know that if I have to let work-related things go, I can; so I do. There are never more than minor repercussions on me. This is tremendous PRIVILEGE.

As I finish this essay, we are in the midst of our 2nd quarantine this month because of COVID exposures. This requires a lot of figuring out and a lot of hard work. But being "privileged doesn't mean you didn't work hard." *It sure doesn't and I sure am* (see Figure 6.1).

Figure 6.1

The COVID Juggle by Ella Theoharis (age 16)

REFERENCE

Ferguson, S. (2014). *Privilege 101: A quick and dirty guide.* Everyday Feminism. Retrieved April 6, 2021, https://everydayfeminism.com/2014/09/what-is-privilege/

CHAPTER 7

ENOUGH

Erica O. Turner

On a weekend in late July, I was sitting with the piles of papers, printouts of tweets and blog posts, and note-filled notebooks I'd been collecting all spread out around me on the round wooden table in our dining room. I was dimly aware that my children, ages 7 months, 7 years and 10 years were in the other room where the older two were on their devices. Usually, this would have irritated and distracted me, and I would have found it difficult to get any work done. But on this day, the typical annoyances were rolling over me.

A couple weeks earlier I had thought that through COVID-19 and the mass uprisings against anti-Black violence, folks had come to better appreciate our interlinked fates. I was cautiously hopeful that we might band together to take care of people, especially children and the communities most marginalized and harmed by the racism and inequality that was plainly on display. But as spring turned into summer, the pandemic had not waned, school leaders had not announced their plans for the fall, and the options seemed to be a potentially unsafe return to school or a continuation of schooling from home. Increasingly, there were signs that some families—especially wealthier families—were securing private solutions to their childcare needs and concerns about their children's safety and education. In the face of the pandemic, it was somewhat tempting to do

Parenting in the Pandemic: The Collision of School, Work, and Life at Home, pp. 31–34
Copyright © 2021 by Information Age Publishing

something similar and to focus on ensuring my own children's needs were met. As an education researcher who studies racial inequality in education, I know that private actions can easily perpetuate inequalities in and out of schools, and as a mother of color, I was thinking about our obligations to other Black and Brown children who do not have the resources that my family does. Retreating into my family's own private world was not the route I wanted to take.

But, while education colleagues were calling out the inequities in news articles and families seemed to recognize they were contributing to an overall system of inequality, I hadn't seen much about what families could do to make schooling more equitable. What, I wondered, are the collective actions we can take to make sure that children and adults, especially those with the fewest resources, can all be safe and learn in the fall? These things were on my mind when the parent group at my children's elementary schools met to discuss equity issues related to virtual schooling, and I volunteered to draft a guide. All of this brought me to the dining room table on that weekend morning.

On a break from that work, I checked Twitter, a new habit developed while both caring for a newborn and searching for insight on a rapidly spreading virus that was not well understood. A tweet in my timeline caught my eye. The writer Connie Schultz had posted two photos side by side. On the left an older photo of a young woman sitting at a typewriter with a baby on her lap. On the right a more recent photo of a young woman speaking into the microphone of a podium while an infant snuggled into a baby carrier she wore. The tweet read:

> 1988: I'm on deadline with baby Cait in my lap. "What am I doing to her?" I used to wonder. 2016: My Cait fights for families, baby Milo strapped to her chest. Feeling guilty about our ambition is such a waste of time. You're doing all that you can. It's enough. #breathe.

I quickly retweeted with my own response. "This made me tear up today ... I've been ignoring my kiddos (dad's in charge) to work on some materials on taking action for equity in pandemic schooling."

No parent is in an easy position right now. The closing of schools as a result of the unchecked spread of COVID-19 has meant that many of us fortunate enough to be able to work from home are constantly with our children, even when we have to work. Suddenly, the old tug-of-war between work and family has reemerged with a vengeance. With little government leadership on the pandemic nor a coherent response to the needs of families with young children, parents and caregivers are left with the preponderance of responsibility for ensuring their families' health and their children's educations in a global health pandemic, and for continuing to work. The stress has been considerable. In my case, even with regular help from my in-laws in caring for my three children while my husband is at work, the ceaseless cycle of waking up, making meal after meal, helping children log on to computers, hounding them to turn in missing assignments or to go outside, answering endless questions, and taking care of a baby, all while only getting a modicum of work done, is immensely frustrating. A few too many times I've lost my composure and ended up yelling at my children, or I have just ignored them. What I have not been doing much is using my time for my children's individual enrichment. I occasionally feel some guilt about that, but the kids are basically doing fine.

In a society where we are expected to give our children our full attention when we are with them and to constantly encourage and nurture their talents, Shultz's tweet was a poignant reminder that focusing on our work instead of our children does not necessarily harm them. In fact, it can be a kind of gift. The tweet brought to mind the years of my own youth spent attending my mother's work fundraisers, events, and meetings. This involved some absorbing of speeches about civil rights and public service, seeing people assemble together to support affirmative action, or fighting against hate acts. It was also a lot of sitting around waiting for these gatherings to end. Reflecting on this, I later added to my tweet, "It's funny because part of what made me teary is that I think it's so important for our children to know about our work. My mother always worked in organizations dedicated to civil rights & education and I was sometimes brought along. I appreciate that deeply."

As I got older, I sometimes took the time when my mother was working to wander around San Francisco's Chinatown where my mother's office was, exploring stores and side alleys, and getting snacks. I had my own adventures, appreciated my city and culture, and enjoyed my independence.

I had not thought about those days in quite a while, but these were mostly fond memories. And, the timing of Shultz's tweet was a welcome reminder, a little jolt of encouragement to forge ahead without feeling guilty about a decision to work.

In just a few hours, I had a first draft of what would become *Equity in Pandemic Schooling: An Action Guide for Families, Educators, & Communities*, a piece of public scholarship to help families, community members and educators to think about how to make schooling more equitable in a deeply inequitable moment, and to urge them to act individually and collectively.

The guide captures—and reflects—a broader set of lessons that I hope my children are learning as our family navigates these times: how we respond to great need; look out for each other and keep each other safe; confront power; show up when, where and how we can; and work collectively and in solidarity for health, education, peace, and justice. In fact, this may be the most important lesson I can help them learn this year, one that I learned from my own mother. And it will not come from my efforts to individually nurture my children, but from them watching me work and understanding what I am trying to do.

I think, for now, it's going to be enough.

CHAPTER 8

SEEKING REFUGE IN TIMES OF CRISIS

Mario Rios Perez

After quarantining for months, my spouse and I accepted a friend's offer to use his cabin over a long weekend. Months had passed since the pandemic had started and we jumped on the opportunity to take a family trip to place that would not put our health at risk. My spouse, three children, and I had been complying with the stay-at-home orders. We had been requesting curbside pick-up, ordering food delivery, and masking-up when we entered public spaces. We followed all COVID-related guidelines. We had accepted the new way of life that was keeping us healthy. The cabin our friend offered was located about a two-hour drive from our home—far enough from the city to give us a break from our quarantined routine. Our friend's offer was too good to pass up, so we packed up and made our way to the cabin.

My spouse and I are both educators—she teaches at a preschool and I at a university. Our experiences in the educational system provided us the opportunity to comfort each over about the common impact the pandemic was having on jobs. We shared tips about the technology we used to teach remotely, discussed the new policies affecting educational institutions, raised questions about best practices in the classroom, and commiserated

Parenting in the Pandemic: The Collision of School, Work, and Life at Home, pp. 35–38
Copyright © 2021 by Information Age Publishing
All rights of reproduction in any form reserved.

over how, as parents and educators, we could continue to send our youngest child (3 years old) to school despite the health recommendations that one of the leading non-pharmaceutical interventions was closing private and public spaces where large groups converged. By early summer, our middle son had participated in a socially distant high school graduation, we had celebrated a major wedding anniversary, I had been promoted to Associate Professor, and we had all attended a Black Lives Matter protest. Given the health risks, we had also suspended our summer travel plans to California where all of our family lives. We found ways to parent, celebrate our accomplishments, and express our dissent in the new environment. By the time we made the trek to the cabin we felt we understood how to remain safe in the broader political and social context. We were confident that the cabin would be a temporary sanctuary, and a good place where our capacity as parents would remain firm.

The cabin was idyllic. Rabbits roamed the grounds, tall pines hugged the cabin, and a sweeping creek wove across the backside. It was the refuge we had all been longing. On the second day we all decided to take a short drive to a grocery store to purchase a few items we forgot to pack. We quickly found what we needed inside the store and headed back to our car. I tried to start the car multiple times, but it did not start. We tinkered with some mechanical parts of the car, with no avail. The day that had started out cool and beautiful, was now scorching and unpredictable. Our main goal was to get our children back to the cabin safely.

In our initial drive into the cabin, we noticed countless "Trump 2020" banners and "Blue Lives Matter" flags staked on the front yards of the rural homes—clear indications to us that white supremacy was brazenly celebrated in these parts of the state. My spouse and I made mention of them but avoided extensive discussion about their presence.

Still stranded, we called for help. Since it was a long weekend, we could not reach a tow-truck company who could come and help us. We made numerous phone calls and hours passed when a sense of despair sunk in. We were afraid of what nightfall might bring. In a last-ditched effort we decided to call the local police department. If anyone, we hoped, they would help us.

I grew up in a Mexican barrio with a history of violent policing, and my experiences with law enforcement are not too pleasant. Despite being a professor, I am still uneasy around anyone wearing a badge. As a brown Chicano, I have one too many stories of unlawful detainment, physical abuse, and negligence. These memories of unjust treatment never leave you. Even with her own fears, my spouse decided it was best for my spouse to call the police. A female operator answered her call, and my wife explained what was happening—we were stranded and needed help getting our children back to our temporary home. A white male police officer showed up about

20 minutes later in an SUV. We all agreed that it was not a good idea for me, a brown man, to ask for help in *Trumplandia*. My spouse served as our family's ambassador. The police officer was curt, cold, and disinterested in providing us any help. Aghast by his indifference and refusal to help, my spouse walked away. I watched from a short distance and entered the conversation just as she paced back to our car. Maybe, just maybe, he will help give my spouse and my youngest child a ride back to the cabin—I thought. I explained our situation, yet again, but he refused to offer any help. "I only give rides to criminals," he said just before he drove off.

As I walked back to the car—stranded, furious, and feeling helpless and emotionally upset—I did not know how I was going to explain to my sons that the police officer—a symbol of public service—had defied his opportunity to help us and, at least momentarily, suspend existing narratives of police oversight. How could my spouse and I make this an educational moment for our sons? We rested, reflected, and continued to collect our thoughts.

Given the recent murders of Breonna Taylor and George Floyd, our dinners had been filled with even more discussions about state violence, police impunity, and social injustice. The story of how we got back to the cabin is too long for this essay—but we did make it back before nightfall. We had dinner—this time without much talk—and sought refuge in our beds later that evening.

Only a few hours later, at around 4:00 A.M., I heard a loud thud. I turned to my bedside, and my spouse was not there. I walked towards the kitchen and was met by my oldest son. We were confused. What was that strong sound? We noticed that the restroom light was on and called out for my spouse, but no answer. We tried opening the door, but it was locked. We gently knocked on the door, and then forcefully pounded on it after there was no response. We kicked in the door and found my spouse motionless on the bathroom floor. Her lips were pale, her body was limp—she was unresponsive. I could not feel a pulse. My son called 911, and before the ambulance arrived, my spouse slowly began to regain her consciousness. My two oldest sons watched on as the paramedics checked her vitals. Was this another educational moment? For the next month or so, doctors struggled to identify what was affecting my spouse. We called 911 three more times after that weekend, and my spouse spent a couple of weeks in the hospital. Only a few days after her last hospitalization, she was back on Zoom with her students who knew nothing of what had transpired that long weekend. She is doing much better now, the doctors concluded it was not COVID related or anything serious. We are hopeful.

These medical hardships and brushings with law enforcement convinced us that our role as parent and educators never ceases. That weekend has become a major talking point for our family. We have examined that weekend through various vantage points. That trip to the cabin did not shelter us from what was happening. In fact, it reminded us of our precarity and vulnerability. In the end, we realized that you can't find refuge in times of crisis.

CHAPTER 9

HOLDING, TRUSTING, AND LOVING IN 2020

Josh Bornstein

It's a little surprising how often leadership advice during the crises of 2020 has paralleled the ways I try to parent. I became both a parent and an elementary teacher in 1988. My children now aged 31, 28, and 13 have given me the most rewarding and most humbling years of my life. In 2020, they engaged the world as a political puppeteer, a humanitarian aid worker, and a middle schooler, respectively. The words "letting go" don't begin to cover how I have had to shed my old ways of parenting: switching from the kind of direct guidance I practiced for decades as an educator and a father to the older two, to being more empathic with all three of them. Now, I strive to hold my children in their pain, rather than fix their problems, and aim to convey my trust in them by telling them that I know they will make the best choices for themselves.

Even so, in the pandemic I have had to make some tough parenting calls. When the adult kids whom I hadn't seen in months, asked if they could come for a visit during a major peak of the pandemic, I was stymied. I definitely wanted nothing more than to spend time, to hold them close, and have them stay over for as long as they wanted. And maybe if I had started our conversation by saying those things, instead of laying out all

Parenting in the Pandemic: The Collision of School, Work, and Life at Home, pp. 39–42
Copyright © 2021 by Information Age Publishing

of the potential risks of social contact, our initial conversation might have gone better. In the end we agreed to gather online. But getting there took a different kind of holding on my part. I needed to risk being vulnerable by sharing how difficult our current situation is for me personally instead of standing at a distance from the emotional aspect and trying to "fix it."

Over the years as a parent and an educator, I have found "holding" in the midst of a child's emotional release, whatever their age may be, is among the most significant and important challenges. I am accustomed to being the level-headed one whom the children turn to for advice and guidance. This year, when we talk through the injustices of pandemic and white supremacy, I find an outlet for that disposition of advisor as we parse how cunning and formidable those forces are, and where my children can find openings for righteous action and loving care.

When loved ones are in pain, I am learning to restrain my impulse to solve their crises in favor of holding the space of calm, comfort, company, and attention. When I was a principal, that was a useful stance too. However, the school community expected a principal who solved problems straightaway, rather than investing the time and trust in the people who actually owned the problem to find the best solution for themselves. In that school atmosphere, I had difficulty keeping my rescuer impulses in check. The school systems I worked in preferred autocrats to democrats, and so I was often in conflict over building the messy and cumbersome democracy that could make our communities more powerful.

Several months into the pandemic, Petriglieri's (2020) definition of "holding" in crisis offered me a satisfying model. He advocated crisis leadership that "contains and interprets what's happening in times of uncertainty," paralleling how adults might care for children. I am no longer a principal, but instead a professor who teaches emerging school leaders. Now, "holding" has meant containing and interpreting the educational ramifications of pandemic and racial justice, and encouraging them to do the same in their schools.

At home, "holding" has meant making space and opportunity for the sadness, rage, disappointment, and despair my kids have borne while we live with quarantine and racial injustice. As their father, I try to be present for their suffering, catharsis, and recovery. The conversations leading to our visit compromise are a solid example.

Professionally, 2020 has been less fraught. Since I identify as a White, cisgendered, straight, upper middle-class, and able-bodied person, I endeavor to hold in my work too. I've found solidarity in two online communities of school leaders (Georgia Leadership Institute for School Improvement, [GLISI] 2020; Solidarity 4 Ed Leaders, 2020). In the first, GLISI's Connected Community (Georgia Leadership Institute for School Improvement, 2020), I encountered the Petriglieri (2020) piece among many others on the social and emotional work of leading in crisis. Frequently, that GLISI group has made insightful links between equity, crisis, family, and school.

I borrowed the GLISI idea to create a workshop of leaders, activists, and academics called Solidarity 4 Ed Leaders (S4EL) (2020) to complement GLISI's work and the plethora of webinars that sprang up in spring and summer. As a working group, those who show up for S4EL seek help and give help as mutual aid. They dive into the complexities of reaching out to families, disrupting our sections of the school-to-prison pipeline, empowering teachers, developing curriculum to meet this moment, and incorporating social and emotional pedagogy for caring and strength rather than compliance.

Both weekly sessions have developed into quasi-familial groups who are clear that going back to business as usual is not an option after 2020 has uncovered systemic injustice and inequity. Participants in the groups trust each other to find openings that make sense locally, and to take time to care for themselves and their communities. I try to do the same with kids, and it seems to me that those weekly gatherings have given me real sustenance to do so.

Finally, I remind myself often that my children, students, colleagues, extended family, friends, and I are all doing the best we can at every moment, even when that's not nearly good enough. When I can embrace that concept, it feels to me like compassion and unconditional love. I'm not always a big enough person to do that, grappling as I do with a hefty predisposition to self-righteousness. But I remain committed to using holding, trusting, and loving as guides for checking that I am being the teacher, leader, and parent I want to be throughout the crisis (see Figure 9.1).

Figure 9.1

Another Morning During COVID by Maya Bornstein (age 14)

REFERENCES

Georgia Leadership Institute for School Improvement. (2020). *Equity consciousness and change leadership.* Connected Community, Virtual.

Petriglieri, G. (2020). The psychology behind effective crisis leadership. *Harvard Business Review.* Retrieved September 1, 2020, from https://hbr.org/2020/04/the-psychology-behind-effective-crisis-leadership

Solidarity 4 Ed Leaders. (2020). *Mutual aid to do the right thing.* Virtual.

CHAPTER 10

HUMANIZING EDUCATION AS OUR WORLD UNRAVELS

Carrie Sampson

In March 2020, my world as I knew it unraveled one piece as a time. I am in my fifth year as a tenure-track assistant professor at Arizona State University. My scholarship lies at the intersections of educational leadership, policy, and equity focused largely on school boards, district structures, and community advocacy. I am a mother of two children who began kindergarten and third grade in Fall 2020 after Arizona reached a spike in COVID-19 cases, becoming one of the worst hotspots for COVID-19 worldwide.

On March 11, 2020, I returned home from a 5-day writing retreat with a fellow mother-scholar. We spent the time writing, sleeping, cooking, storytelling, and laughing. This was the last time I got a massage and enjoyed a dine-in meal at a restaurant before the pandemic hit. Although my friend and I knew the pandemic was coming our way, we did not fully realize the impact COVID would have on our day-to-day lives once we returned home.

The first piece to unravel was schools going online. After "Spring Break," my 4-year-old son's preschool closed, and my 7-year old daughter's elementary school went virtual, which I describe later in more detail. To date, my kids have not returned to in-person school. The in-person graduate course I taught transitioned to Zoom. We were left to learn how

Parenting in the Pandemic: The Collision of School, Work, and Life at Home, pp. 43–47

to navigate the chaos of both schooling and work in our bedrooms, living room, and kitchen.

The second piece to unravel was our family's strict lockdown. As the stories of people dying of COVID-19 escalated and got closer to home, I became highly concerned about my mother who lived with us, and who at 69-years old and a smoker, was considered high risk for COVID. So we bought extra food and toilet paper, then bunkered down for what we thought might be several weeks at most.

Then came the third piece to unravel … our family being hit by COVID. At the end of March, my aunt in Arizona became the first confirmed case of COVID in our family. Eleven of my family members lived in her home. Although they survived, several of them became really ill and suspected they had COVID but could not access testing. By mid-April, COVID struck our New York family. My 89-year-old grandmother-in-law was admitted to the hospital, spent nearly a week there, and died without family by her side. I witnessed, in despair, as my husband broke down in uncontrollable tears when the doctor called to explain her deteriorating health. During the call, the doctor put my husband on hold while he tried but failed to resuscitate her as she coded again for the third and final time. Like thousands of other families throughout the world, *we attended my grandmother-in-law, Doreen Ometa Seale's funeral on Zoom.* Soon after, we learned that my mother-in-law also had COVID. From Arizona, we set up Instacart to send her groceries in Brooklyn, NY and prepared ourselves for the possibility of continued loss. Luckily, she survived.

In late May, our world was rocked again by the horrendous murders of George Floyd, Breonna Taylor, and Ahmaud Arbery. I invited my children to join my mother and me at the kitchen table to make protest signs— "Stop Killing Our Children," "Black Lives Matter," and "No Justice, No Peace"—while I explained to them what happened, why Black people are being killed, and why we must protest these injustices even in the midst of COVID.

The latest of my world unraveling was the passing of my mother. As COVID hit its peak in July, my mother became ill. After making hundreds of phone calls to avoid the crowded emergency rooms, I secured out-of-patient testing. Test results sent her to the hospital. The no visitor policy due to COVID meant I had to drop her off twice at the hospital alone for several days. She was diagnosed with a rare and aggressive cancer. When she returned home, I took care of her by myself since COVID made it too risky for others to help. As she deteriorated, medical staff gave me two options: send her back to the hospital alone or send her to hospice where limited family visits (masked) were allowed. I opted for the latter. She died in mid-August the night before my children's first day school's Fall semester. I waited until their Zoom live lesson ended to share the heartbreaking news with them that their Nana, who they loved dearly, passed away. A week later, a small group of us attended her funeral in-person, wearing masks and unable to hug each other, while the rest of our family and friends watched online.

As I walk through these horrendous moments and think about the role of education in our lives, I wonder: What does it mean to humanize schooling? Better yet, what does it mean to humanize teaching and learning for *all* children *and* their families? As a mother-scholar whose research focuses on educational equity, the pandemic of COVID has forced me to reckon with these questions concerning the role schools play in the betterment of humanity. And as a Black and Chicana woman raised in a working-class family in both rural and urban environments, the pandemics of racism, sexism, and classism that are now layered with COVID-19 has re-centered my questions about what a humanizing education means in terms of social justice and emancipation, and whether schools will ever embody that, especially for our Black, Indigenous, and People of Color (BIPOC) children and families.

I have grown tremendously over the last several months. I have come to a deeper understanding of who I am, what's important in this lifetime, and what I hope to contribute that might last beyond me. As a mother and education scholar who is grappling to answer these questions concerning humanity and schooling, I offer three ideas.

1. "Partnering with families was crucial before this pandemic, and is even more crucial now."

This above quote is from an email I sent my daughter's school principal about four weeks into the shift to online learning. Pre-COVID, I was in conversations with school and district leaders at my daughter's predominately Black and Brown school about both engaging families and employing an asset-based perspective of families. Before COVID, the school made several major decisions without consulting families and I had overheard teachers' deficit-oriented comments about parents' lack of knowledge, skills, and concern for their children's education. School and district leaders offered me lukewarm responses—a pat on the back and little action.

When the school shifted online during COVID, school and district leaders maintained the same lack of engagement. Weeks passed and they never solicited feedback from families, not even a simple survey to get a sense of what was working well or not for families who were all of sudden tasked with managing their children's schooling from home. In conversations with other mothers of color near me, I learned that their experience was similar. Frustrated, the four of us coauthored an *essay urging schools and districts to engage families*.

Schools' willingness and ability to authentically engage families in teaching and learning of youth was critical before COVID, during COVID, and beyond COVID. This pandemic simply highlighted the need for engaging families because, for the most part, schooling had shifted to families' homes.

2. Culturally sustaining teaching and learning go beyond the walls of schools.

Education isn't confined to classrooms and schools. We are surrounded by opportunities to teach and learn from each other. Learning happens during play, interactions, storytelling, cooking, and cleaning. During this pandemic, I have witnessed the beauty of my children's creativity, often when they hit the height of their boredom. They are building forts in our living room, organizing concerts in our dining room, and simulating coffee shops in our kitchen. They are leading social clubs and talent shows with friends via Zoom and spending lots of time outdoors experimenting with gardens, ladybugs, and sports.

The pandemic inspired us to invite strangers, friends, and our family into our home, virtually, to offer our kids relevant and engaging curriculum. At the beginning of COVID shutdown, Ms. Sonia Lewis, a former teacher from Sacramento, California and someone I have never met, offered a Black-centered social studies course called Teach-In Time for Revolutionary Minds via Facebook. Every Tuesday and Thursday for 90-minutes, my 7-year-old daughter joined about 10 other youth her age from across the U.S. via Zoom to learn about Black-centered historical moments and leaders. Moreover, when protests against racial injustice escalated over the summer, Ms. Sonia facilitated the opportunity for our kids to reflect, discuss, and understand what was happening.

We also invited family members to share their knowledges about subjects, such as my cousin who could teach my kids about being body positive and my actor/singer sister-in-law who gave voice lessons. These experiences, along with other daily life lessons my children and I embark on, have reminded me that we are always learning, and schools are often simply one small piece of a whole myriad of this learning that occurs.

3. Educators must humanize the process of teaching and learning.

Many of us have experienced devastating trials and losses during this pandemic. This time made it incredibly apparent that educators must approach teaching and learning in the most humane way possible.

When schools first went online, I sat next to my daughter and overheard the ways that her teacher spoke to her and her peers in her class. Despite the fact that many families were in the middle of chaos, she made many disparaging comments about the kids going to sleep too late at night, wearing their pajamas during the Google classroom sessions, questioning why they hadn't done projects that required printing, and pointing out who she thought was smart or not. Each day, my daughter grew increasingly unengaged while I grew increasingly frustrated with the negativity, lack of empathy, and judgement that this teacher spewed. During one of the sessions and after overhearing the teachers' rude comment, I directed my daughter to logout of class. She didn't return for the rest of the year.

Meanwhile, my daughter's former teacher invited her to a virtual lunch date. There was nothing more exciting that came from this school during this timeframe than the virtual lunch where she and this teacher connected for 30 minutes. Similarly, in the Revolutionary Minds course, which my daughter attended from April through August, Ms. Sonia, a Black woman and a mother of two children in the course, taught in a humanizing manner. Not only did she offer a culturally relevant curriculum, she checked-in with students, engaged them in dialogue, inserted breaks that included songs and dances of the kids' choice, and was in constant back and forth communication with families. When I asked my daughter why she wanted to continue the course, she said because she loves learning about Black history since she never gets to learn about it in school and she loves Ms. Sonia. Although it was disheartening to experience the dehumanization in school, it was incredibly exciting to witness how humanizing education can be when educators come from a place of authentic connection, care, and love.

As we move forward and hopefully into a world where COVID is not controlling so much of what is going on with schools, the pandemic of racism, sexism, classism and all the other isms will remain. The three ideas I offer us to consider more deeply in education—partnering with families, digging into the teaching, and learning that occurs beyond schools, and humanizing schooling—were ideas that existed before COVID and will hopefully exist more prominently after COVID.

CHAPTER 11

THE WAYS WE PARENTED

Decoteau J. Irby

We told ourselves they don't need to know what's going on. We parented to give our children, four and seven at the time, as normal a life as possible. About two months prior to the May 2020 uprisings, city officials abruptly closed Chicago Public Schools. Park district employees plastered city playgrounds with "Closed due to Covid-19" signs. Religious leaders canceled services. Business owners closed their doors. But we still had the normalcy of our neighborhood and our home. We rode bikes. We frequented our local park. We blew bubbles. We roamed blocks we had never walked, stared at the intricate architecture of centuries old houses, and exchanged waves with kids who stared at us from the safety of their homes. We visited neighbors without giving them prior notice. "We're on your block. Are you home?" I texted. I knew they probably were. The stay-at-home order was in full effect. While we adults chatted from a distance, our children raced along the sidewalk.

We parented with courage. Minneapolis police officers murdered George Floyd. Eight minutes. Around the clock, protesters overwhelmed cities throughout the world. Flames engulfed downtowns that a month earlier sat desolate, decimated by stay-at-home orders and fears of Covid-19. In downtown Chicago, protesters demanded justice for George Floyd, Ahmaud Arbery, Breonna Taylor, and Elijah Mclain and Sandra Bland and

Parenting in the Pandemic: The Collision of School, Work, and Life at Home, pp. 49–51
Copyright © 2021 by Information Age Publishing

Corey Stingley, and Emmett Till, and … Chicago's city officials safeguarded the Loop shopping district, upscale Magnificent Mile and the white affluent Northside. Mayor Lori Lightfoot ordered bridges over the Chicago river lifted. Police vehicles blocked freeway routes leading north. The Chicago sanitation department used their fleet to blockade northbound residential streets. If you must loot, burn, and riot … do it on the Southside. Plumes of smoke streamed upward. The wind blew. Smoke filled our house. Alas, we told ourselves they need to know what's going on.

We parented to open our children's eyes to hard facts of racism. We walked our children down our burnt out looted neighborhood commercial corridor. With masks over our faces, we stared at the casualties of our country's longstanding and most insidious pandemic. We explained to them what happened. They asked why. We explained. They asked why. We offered yet more candid explanations of why we don't trust the police, the reasons why people looted stores, and burned properties. We watched neighbors board-up, clean-up, rebuild, and beautify. The protests grew. As the bubble we worked so hard to create for our children slowly deflated we affirmed that our Black lives were precious and worthy of everything good. We marched. We talked. We bought Black.

We parented to give our children joy in the pandemics. We tried to remote learn. Chicago Public Schools failed. Schools everywhere failed. We grew frustrated. I slowly gave up. Grades be damned. I settled for incompletes. We frequented our local park. We disagreed about what exactly we should be doing. Structure or no structure? Our children played out front in the sprinkler. They screamed with delight. Passersby smiled and crossed the street. We always ate lunch at 12:00. Then 2:00. Then 1:15. Normalcy was over. We painted our porch. We repaired our dilapidated wooden fence, painted, and stenciled it with bright yellow, blue, and white flowers and handprints. Fence completed, my partner transformed our garage into an outdoor oasis, complete with AstroTurf, curtains, and a string of butterfly lights. We camped in the garage. A raccoon camped in the garage. While I flushed the raccoon out with a water hose, our children stood on the porch and screamed with fearful delight, rooting for my victory. They gave mommy a play-by-play reenactment. We laughed hard.

We parented with fear. We watched as 300,000 people's lives were snatched away, waiting breath held, for COVID-19 to visit our own families. We canceled our traditional summer trips to South Carolina. We missed our families. I juggled my demanding academic job. At home, I tried to keep some sort of daily schedule. I tried to keep up with login credentials for remote learning for a second time. I failed again. My partner, a physician assistant, noticed I was struggling. She resigned from her job, an overburdened neighborhood health clinic that became overwhelmed during the first COVID-19 pandemic spike. I was elated because I feared

Covid-19 was waiting to infect her. I feared the police. I feared the uptick in carjacking and violent crime sweeping the city. I feared for my children. I feared they would get sick from playing on the swing set. I scolded them for asking. In time, they acted as though the playground didn't exist. One day, they asked again. I relented. My partner was angry that I let them. I wanted their futures to not be this. Fearing I was too far past my contract deadline, I started back working on my book. The stress caused my temper to shorten. Part of my beard stopped growing. I submitted the book—eight months late.

We parented to cultivate responsibility. We limited television. We assigned chores. Our 5-year-old took great pride in his responsibility to water the plants. Our 7-year-old agreed to prepare lunch. She didn't do it. Then she agreed to tidy the basement. She didn't do it. When we rode bicycles, mommy insisted we wear helmets. We picked up trash and maintained our neighborhood park because the park district employees were furloughed. We worked our block club garden. We grilled. We prepared healthy meals. We watched television. We Zoomed. We phoned. We Face Timed. We walked or played basketball before the school day began. We completed the required assignments. We voted. We waited. We won. We thanked God. We prayed. We wrote short stories and songs. We snapped photos. We stayed home. We told ourselves that years from now, they will need to know what went on.

SECTION II

"GOT TO GO THROUGH IT!":
SCHOOLING AT HOME

We're going on a bear hunt.

We're going to catch a big one.

What a beautiful day!

We're not scared.

Uh-uh!

Mud

Thick oozy mud

We can't go over it.

We can't go under it.

We can't go around it.

Oh no!

We've got to go through it!

—Traditional camp song and picture book (Rosen, 2003)

As COVID spread across the country, school after school after school shut down. All of a sudden school was now happening in our homes. Very young children, elementary age kids, adolescents and young adults along with their parents were now making school at home--from kitchens, backyards, bedrooms, closets. As much as we wanted, as much as parents might have wished, as much as many kids would have preferred, there was no way around it, over it or under it—school was happening in our homes. "We've got to go through it."

As we have moved through the pandemic, some schools brought children back to school; some schools have a mix of in person and remote learning, and some schools are still fully remote. Some families have spent the year outside the school system, no longer tethered to traditional schooling. Others have gotten more involved in their schools than ever before, consulting on reopening plans and advising teachers learning to teach online. This section includes stories from across those realities and is organized roughly chronologically by children's age. Beginning with young children, progressing into adolescence and ending with young adults, these parents offer a glimpse of their experience as they engaged in schooling at home.

With our children's education colliding with our educator selves, we have called on our professional expertise in different ways to help us navigate the array of decisions schooling at home demands. In so doing, we are confronted with bringing our educational philosophies to life at the same time that our perspectives shift by engaging in our children's learning so intimately. The essays in this section illustrate how both our expertise shapes our experience and our experience adds to our expertise. In these reflections on the highs and lows of learning at home, the essays in this section reveal the insights gained as we have worked to "go through it."

CHAPTER 12

MAMÃE

Gabrielle Oliveira

Mamãe, mamãe, mamãe. I hear these words nonstop as I finally sit down on my laptop to answer one e-mail. *Just one e-mail* I think to myself. If you answer this one e-mail, maybe you will get closer to answering all of the others that are sitting in your inbox, piling up right before your eyes. My two boys, 6 and 3, are the little loves of my life. I wouldn't trade watching them do things, learn and play for anything in the world. Except. Well, except for the fact that I need to keep my job and that I love my job. Sociologist Jessica Calarco in an interview said "Other countries have social safety nets. The U.S. has women."[1] And yes, while I sit and try to answer one e-mail or finish one call or for once turn on my camera on zoom, I still hear the words: *Mamãe, mamãe, mamãe, I want water, can you read to me, can you play with me, can you … I want you to … please … help me with ….* And I feel that familiar feeling of guilt, love and frustration all muddled up into one. There is no pause or fast forward button as a parent, but there is also no rewind. We have to go through it. *Together.*

When quarantine hit in March, my partner and I came up with a schedule while the kids were home full time and both of us were expected to work and produce *normally*. There were two shifts: 9 A.M. to 2 P.M. and 2 P.M.—6 P.M. We could usually negotiate those early hours of 6:30—8:30 A.M. depending on who needed more sleep, more time to make a phone

Parenting in the Pandemic: The Collision of School, Work, and Life at Home, pp. 55–59

call, time to go grocery shopping etc. I usually took the morning into afternoon shift because my schedule was a lot more flexible. I didn't have to be in meetings with clients or coordinate team efforts in order to keep a business afloat. I still had my research and writing to do, though. I also took the longer shift because deep down I thought I could work with both kids more effectively, since the youngest napped in the afternoon. I am a micromanager, a scheduler, a planner. On a normal day I think about my research, my teaching, but also what I will make for dinner, who needs underwear and if we have enough garbage bags. I convinced myself and others around me that I could, somehow, work and write for four hours straight after being with my two kids for the previous 6 hours. By the time I hit my computer at 2:15 p.m. I was exhausted. I wanted a nap, maybe some reality TV. I wanted so badly to keep my research going, continue to interview folks, conduct online observations of classrooms, but I could see myself getting more and more tired. By the end of April, I was operating at minimum capacity and feeling conflicted about wanting to do both at the same time: work and take care of my children.

It didn't help that I knew of male colleagues who were actually enjoying the "downtime" they had to read, write and reflect. Maybe even take on a new hobby. A hobby! My partner and I are a team. I consider myself lucky and privileged to have a job that allowed flexibility, an incredible partner and healthy children. However, the feeling of falling behind, being out of the game and simply put *failing* never left me.

April, May and June were tough. The days, weeks and months became increasingly hard. My 3-year-old wanted to play. But my kindergartner still had to do a lot of school work and join zooms, and do math. Turns out having a PhD really doesn't help you teach your kindergartener how to read, add or subtract.

There were the silver linings. We also came up with a lot of little rituals, like our morning walks where we would look for "evidence" as to if animals had been there. Bird poop was always a hit and my kids would scream "evidence" at the sight of the white stains on the ground! My then 5-year-old learned to ride a bike without wheels, my then 2-year-old who was a little late to talk, was chatting up a storm. We cooked through three cookbooks, we did science observations and let's be real: we watched TV. We had birthdays, anniversaries and celebrated our families in Brazil and California via zoom. We missed births, weddings, hugs, graduations, and baptisms. Right after my oldest turned 6 he had his last day in kindergarten. His teacher, on zoom, called each name in their classroom and when it was his turn, she went: "Goodbye Kindergarten Jack, Hello First Grader." I sobbed next to him. I was such an emotional wreck. I kept thinking again about all of the guilt I felt about wanting to work, write, research while these little creatures were going through a lot in their own little lives. "Mamãe, is this our life now?", asked my 6-year-old.

When summer rolled around I felt a sense of relief. I didn't have to do the school work anymore with my children and maybe we could go outside, swim, explore. In late July and August my kids were able to do outdoor camp. They were so hungry to be with other kids that putting masks on was never a battle. I slowly felt like I was getting my groove back. I started to write more. During all of these months I kept in touch with all of the participants in the research I had started in the year prior. Yes, in part because my neoliberal academic brain would not leave my body, but also because immigrant parents in my research were actively teaching me what it felt like to be away from loved ones. Then, all of my zoom interruptions, all of the times I heard "Mamãe, mamãe, mamãe" I kept thinking, *I will miss this time together.*

September came and school was back in session: hybrid models, masks, social distancing, hand sanitizers and new social norms of sharing space. It felt like we were all as a family still emerging from a dystopic time. In so many ways my children kept me sane during these months. I had to provide them with a routine and with a sense of safety that I myself could not get from my work. I compared myself with other parents who I thought "had it together"—but maybe they didn't really have it all together either. I compared myself with other scholars who I thought "were being so productive"—but maybe they weren't that productive either. I felt like I gave it my all, all of my energy and resilience during the spring. Would I still have anything left in the fall?

The thing is about parenting: there is always more from where that came from. And as I read the book "We Are Going On a Bear Hunt" (Rosen, 2003) to my children at night, I adopted the mantra the family repeats every other page on that book: "We can't go over it, we can't go under it, we have to go through it."

Figure 12.1

My Rainbow Year by Jack (age 6) and Noah (age 3)

Figure 12.2

My Rainbow Year 2 by Jack (age 6) and Noah (age 3)

REFERENCE

Rosen, M. (2003). *We are going on a bear hunt*. Simon & Schuster.

NOTE

1. https://annehelen.substack.com/p/other-countries-have-social-safety

CHAPTER 13

CAROUSEL PARENTING

Up, Down, and Around We Go Again

Jacob Hall

Originally known as the Carousel Center, the Syracuse mall is home to an iconic, 111-year-old carousel (Moriarty, 2020). My 3 and 5-year-old sons eagerly await a ride each time our family visits the mall, yet the COVID-19 pandemic has brought the gentle circling of hand painted horses, their rolling ups and downs, and their quintessential melody to a silent halt. While this may be trivial to some, it is the incessant compounding of such trivialities which created difficulties for my wife and I as we parented young children during the pandemic. It is leaving preschool for spring break and never returning to see your friends again or to say goodbye to your first teacher. It is your out of state grandparents cancelling their visit at the last minute due to new travel bans. It is playground after playground wrapped in caution tape, waving at your quarantined friends through the window, and realizing that adult church is much different than the canceled children's programming. It is the long-awaited birthday party streamed on Zoom, living with stressed and overworked parents, and learning, as my 5-year-old has, to summarize these disappointments with a sigh and an "Oh, it's the virus."

The Carousel Strategy, when students rotate around the classroom and stop at various stations, has been used for cooperative learning, reviewing concepts, activating prior knowledge, reflecting on learning, and showcasing artifacts (Allen, n.d.). My wife and I attempted to adopt a similar rhythm to balancing our pandemic parenting and working. After both our jobs in higher education schools of education transitioned us to sharing a makeshift office at home, I would begin the day between 4:00–5:00 A.M. with writing manuscripts, responding to e-mails, and grading student work. Breakfast served as a transition when my wife went to work in the home office, and I began parenting. For the first few weeks of pandemic parenting, I attempted a modified preschool curriculum in the morning that would hopefully engage both boys. Lunchtime brought us together for a few minutes, followed by naptime for the youngest, solo play time for the oldest, and back to work for both my wife and I as long as the peace could persist. Once the afternoon lull subsided, we negotiated the final stops on our work/life carousel to accommodate deadlines and meetings. All this seemed to be going well for a couple weeks, until we realized the COVID-19 parenting carousel had no definitive end in sight; we needed off or we needed longer, more purposeful stops at the stations. We needed resting points and moments for reflection.

While these moments for reflection were most commonly a family walk or conversation with my wife as the boys played in the backyard, I fondly recall a rather irregular, hour-long road trip to a grocery store. Desperately needing to leave home for some physical and mental distancing from the home space that had become work, school, church, and play, we spontaneously dropped everything one afternoon for this trip. It had been some time since the boys had really gone anywhere, and their excitement to sit in the car for an hour was unmistakable. Enjoying the grocery getaway so much, we extended it by walking around a historic park situated on Lake Ontario. Walking the quiet paths around the park and watching the boys explore reminded me of their love of the outdoors and the creativity in their play. Each encounter with the various 1800s-era cannons scattered around the park came with a series of questions about information on the placard, the projected distance, and guesses about why some shot farther than others. In this instance of rest and reflection, I observed their inquisitiveness and their vibrant engagement with this experience and pondered how these moments could be reintegrated in the everyday pandemic carousel.

"No, I don't want to do school today!" my eldest bellowed in a moment of heartfelt honesty. I was taken aback by this attitude as he had previously loved school, and I had always viewed myself as an exemplary educator. I battled a feeling of failure and resentment. Amidst the ever-growing pile of work expectations and keeping track of my 2-year-old, I had tried to replicate a preschool experience. We were having morning meetings;

incorporating free play, station time and multimodal experiences; integrating music and art; and attempting to involve a 2-year-old as a fellow knowledge constructor. Trying to be patient, I asked him what he wanted to do instead of school. "I want to build," he replied. "Build what?" I asked in frustration. He wanted to build anything: forts that used every blanket and pillow in the house, animal habitats made of Lego bricks, car garages with magnetic tiles, jeeps, and balls from piles of Brainflakes, and a homemade swimming pool by digging a wide hole in the sandbox that was then covered in tarp. As I listened to all these ideas come pouring from my 5-year-old, I realized that he did not want to do school as I had constructed it. In my haste to fabricate a child-centered learning space, I forgot about the child for whom I should have been constructing the space. My concern with schedule and running the work/life carousel had consumed me; I had neglected my deepest held beliefs about teaching.

Curiosity, play, and sociability, the "impulses that help children learn and direct their own learning" (Mehta et al., 2020, p. 685), had been central to my pedagogy and parenting practices. Somewhere along the shift to learning from home and my attempts to control an element of the pandemic experience, I lost sight of curiosity, play, and sociability. Looking for simple solutions, I reviewed communication from my son's school. His preschool teacher sent emails with lists of tasks children could complete, and the school district provided a TV guide of local PBS programming. They too, appeared to be struggling for ways to support parents of young children learning at home. None of what was sent home matched my son's desire to build—to be creative. Determined to re-center creativity, we re-imagined preschool from home.

Although it presented several challenges (e.g. increasing time commitment, better facilitating out-of-the-box, child-driven ideas, and cleaning mud, paint, or cooking messes between meetings), I reorganized the preschool at home experience to emphasize opportunities for play and building—constructing knowledge and tangible artifacts (Papert & Harel, 1991). A primary hurdle in this new routine was the time-consuming role of modeling, structuring, and facilitating play (Mehta et al., 2020). Whereas the prior preschool routine had intermittent moments for quick e-mail replies, engaging in the play, encouraging dialogue, and prompting reflection demanded more attention. As a parent and an educator, however, the time was worth the investment as it was rewarding to see my children's responses and exciting to think of new possibilities for play and learning. Each day focused on a single child-proposed adventure such as searching for flora and fauna in the woods, dissecting chestnuts to examine why squirrels like to eat them so much, and reenacting successful rescue missions with an assortment of imaginary characters. Sometimes the adventures were so good we went on them more than once. While pandemic parenting never became easy, emphasizing play and creativity were essential to providing us with more ups than downs on the work/life carousel.

Figure 13.1

Backyard Adventures by Jimmy (age 6)

REFERENCES

Allen, C. (n.d.). *Brainstorming and reviewing using the carousel strategy*. ReadWriteThink. Retrieved November 9, 2020, from http://www.readwritethink.org/professional-development/strategy-guides/brainstorming-reviewing-using-carousel-30630.html

Mehta, R., Henriksen, D., Mishra, P., & Deep-Play Research Group. (2020). "Let the children play!": Connecting evolutionary psychology and creativity with Peter Gray. *TechTrends, 64*, 684–689.

Moriarty, R. (2020). *Destiny USA's antique carousel isn't spinning. Here's why*. Syracuse.Com. https://www.syracuse.com/business/2020/07/destiny-usas-antique-carousel-isnt-spinning-heres-why.html

Papert, S., & Harel, I. (1991). Situating Constructionism. *Constructionism*, 1–11. https://doi.org/10.1111/1467-9752.00269

CHAPTER 14

REALTIME RUMINATIONS

Young Children's Thoughts on
Social Life in 2020

Ariana Mangual Figueroa

One of the last articles I published before the coronavirus pandemic began was an essay in response to the Presidential Address that Thea Abu El-Haj delivered to the Council of Anthropology and Education (CAE) during the 2018 American Anthropological Association meeting. As I sat to write this essay late in November of 2020, I was also facilitating virtual CAE sessions replacing the in-person annual meeting typically held during that same week. My 2019 essay—Allá Sobre el Horizonte/There Over the Horizon—serves as my entry point here because it makes the case that visual metaphors, like lines and circles, help us all make sense of the complexity of social relationships. For example, straight lines can indicate thresholds delineating social boundaries between people. Meanwhile, circles can denote social reproduction or refer to models of grassroots organizing used in struggles for justice.

In the early days of the pandemic when the mayor of New York City declared a state of emergency, the salience of thresholds was stronger

Parenting in the Pandemic: The Collision of School, Work, and Life at Home, pp. 65–71
Copyright © 2021 by Information Age Publishing

than usual. The everyday sounds of people commuting to school and work were replaced with the constant sounds of ambulance sirens. March 13 was the last day that my daughters attended school in person and by March 16 all New York City public schools were shuttered for the remainder of the academic year. For over a month, no one in my household crossed any thresholds. None of us passed through the doorway from inside to outside. Yet, even as the divide between inside and outside was the strongest I have ever known, the boundaries between school and home were collapsing. As parents, we were responsible for managing our children's formal schooling in new ways in the absence of in-person learning at school.

My husband Ben suggested that I chronicle this time and I called my journal *Homebound Homeschool*. The second half of this essay draws on excerpts from a total of 105 journal entries that include the 75 days of school and 15 weekends that we shared from March 13 to June 26 (the last day of the NYC public school calendar). Ben was so right to encourage me to write—as a teacher, it helped me to have a reflective practice; as a mother, it made it possible to gain space when there was no break in parenting; and as an ethnographer, it prompted me to listen in new ways to the familiar voices of my own children. I jotted down what I heard as my daughters, Lucía and Marcela, made sense of quarantine, of the limited threshold crossings (between home and school, inside and outside), and of their own metaphors for social relationships and collective action.

Thresholds/Dichotomies

Throughout the pandemic Lucía and Marcela have asked a lot of threshold questions expressing concern about the state of existing social boundaries that they are familiar with. During the early months of quarantine they asked, for example: *when were we in real school versus homeschool? Would we ever go outside or would we have to stay inside? Would we be able to go to the pool or Coney Island during the summer?* These questions were largely dichotomous questions meriting an either/or answer. This didn't mean that they were superficial—in fact, they were very emotionally laden—but it did mean that they had fairly simple answers, at least during the early period from March through May 2020. And it didn't mean that the process of arriving at those answers was simple for Ben and I; still the answers we shared with the girls did not always allude to the more complicated reckoning we were constantly doing between the often-incompatible logics of desire and risk. These questions always provided insight into what is on the girls' minds: what thresholds did they want to cross or not? What milestones did they long for?

The following two entries from *Homebound Homeschool* represent the girls' thinking about temporal, spatial, and social thresholds in the pandemic last spring.

Day 5, March 19

As the girls were getting into bed, choosing their pajamas and bedtime books, Lucía asked to borrow something soft to cover her stuffies with. In the last week or so she's wanted to sleep with a sweatshirt or t-shirt of mine. We went to get one out of my closet and Marcela asked that I bring her one too. Pleased with the oversized cotton t-shirt I lent her, Marcela asked if she could wear it to school one day. I replied: *sí, a homeschool.* I sensed a little tremble in her voice as Marcela asked: *no, when are we going to real school again?* I said: *en un rato, vamos a tener homeschool por ahora.* Lucía, in a knowledgeable eldest voice, said: *probably a month.*

Within a week of quarantine, the girls had started to grapple with boundaries—those that were newly erected and those that were collapsing. This included the thresholds between real and home school, between the present and (what to them seemed like a distant) future, and even between their clothing and mine.

Nearly two months after quarantine began, we started taking short family walks through our neighborhood and the girls often ruminated on the new protocols we were all adjusting to.

Day 29, April 22

As we prepared to leave one morning, putting on our masks and bandanas, Marcela explained: *we have to wear our masks now when we go out because of the virus.* Lucía added: *which is so annoying!* I explained that we would practice social distancing from our neighbors even though it would still be nice to wave to them. Lucía specified, *yeah not 6 feet,* wondering out loud as she stretched out her arms wide and arched her head back: *what if we had a playdate and we had to stay like this far away?*

Pandemic life continues to raise questions about connection in spite of distance. Even now as we adhere to basic rules of thumb, it's difficult to come to terms with maintaining distance from loved ones: family, friends, and neighbors alike.

Ultimately, these thresholds have a lot to do with feeling agentic or powerless in this moment. With every milestone that approaches—a new school year, celebrating birthdays, the upcoming holidays—we find new ways of coping with pandemic life and we continue to register how deeply we are still in this reality. At the time of writing, the NYC Department of Education drastically changed its policy for parental decision-making regarding their children's mode of instruction: shifting from offering parents multiple moments in the school year to switch between remote and in-person learning to providing only one opportunity to change their enrollment status. The deadline to reach a decision and to submit this essay fell on the same day, reminding me that writing through the moments of pandemic life when I feel the limits of my agency continues to provide much-needed opportunities for reflection and sense-making.

Collectives/Circles

For many months, and sometimes even now, the boundaries between people, institutions, and places feel stronger than ever. But in some ways, possibilities for another kind of sociality have become possible. As we moved into the late-spring and summer of 2020, the girls began to evoke a different view of sociality that was not so dichotomous. As an ethnographer looking for patterns—and breaks in patterns—this shift shows up in my journal as we began to have open conversations at home about the police murder of George Floyd, the Black Lives Matter movement, and our collective responsibility. In early June, as uprisings took place in central parts of Brooklyn, our family attended two consecutive nights of collective action to bring visibility to the Black Lives Matter movement within our neighborhood. The girls began to evoke circles as they represented experiences of taking grassroots political action and thinking through race and racism. Interestingly, as they took up these complex questions, I noticed that they began drawing on visual resources to represent their ideas visually as they talked (see Figure 14.1).

At the neighborhood gathering for Black Lives Matter, Marcela drew as we held signs, played drums, and waved to those honking horns as they drove by. From her 5-year-old point of view, she drew what she saw: *two people inside a circle surrounded by shoes*. This drawing is itself straddles two modes of representation: an inner area with two people standing—perhaps her and Lucía—and a larger circle made up of the shoes ensconcing the two inside.

Figure 14.1

Day 58, June 3

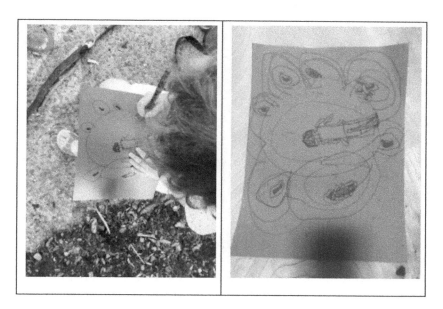

A week after attending the local actions in our neighborhood, as we continued conversations about state violence, social movements, and our roles at home, Lucía turned to beading and created a narrative out of a necklace she'd created (Figure 14.2). She explained: *there are a few people on this side who are not safe. And there are more of us, the rest of the beads, who are.* To which I added: *so we have a responsibility to lift up and stand with everyone so that we can all be safe.* Lucía countered: *we're separated by this knot* (the one she herself tied earlier to close the loop of the necklace). Reaching out to hold the necklace, I offered an alternative: *if we move your finger then we all come together, we are all connected and stronger.* As she moved her finger to let the necklace hang around her neck, she seemed compelled by this idea of connection, of strength in a circle. Lucía's comments about the knot and the separation between us recalled for me the lyrics to the Soledad Bravo song published in the essay mentioned at the opening of this reflection.

Figure 14.2

Days 69 and 70, June 18 and 19

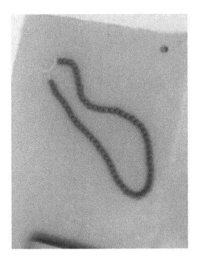

The following day, I observed Lucía playing with tiny smooth rocks on her bed, just moments before a Zoom school morning meeting in which the children would share out their beliefs about justice and their stories of attending local grassroots actions in the previous weeks. While she played, I heard Lucía narrating that rocks of different colors didn't have to remain in separate piles but could become friends and play together. As she moved the rocks closer, crossing an imaginary line we may call race and racism, she grouped them into a circle on her bed (Figure 14.3).

Figure 14.3

Lucía Playing With Tiny Smooth Rocks on Her Bed

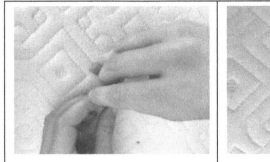

Our multilingual, interracial family lives out this principle, as do so many other parts of Lucía's life which she is aware of and names (*if it wasn't for Ruby Bridges, so-and-so wouldn't be my teacher*). The collection of colorful rocks huddled together in one spot evoked the circle that Marcela had drawn just the week before, and Lucía's statement explicitly rejected any notion of segregation based upon differences in color. Her evocation of Ruby Bridges reflects her understanding that Black activists—and children's actions—constitute brave attempts at realizing the tenets of a life we can imagine (and still struggle to realize) today.

CHAPTER 15

SOCIAL ISOLATION WHILE
SELF-ISOLATING

Shaun M. Dougherty

The good news is that parenting always carries an element of the unexpected, so pandemic parenting did not catch me entirely unaware. However, in our household, like all those with children, there are big differences in the routines, affect, and balance of needs that we must work to meet on a daily basis.

The hardest part for me was not knowing what to tell my kids about when we can go back to normal, and worrying that we won't know how to do that once the opportunity is available to us again. In a house where one of the adults has bad asthma that has been worsened by local allergens (in a place we are still new to discovering), the focus on minimizing risk and exposure has been central.

Time is both fast and slow. Monday morning can feel like a week getting a first and third grader fed, logged into their computer, and engaged enough to learn. Let alone responding to the realization that folders and materials have mysteriously moved over the weekend. Bedrooms are now for sleeping, learning, and playing, which has blurred the line between all of these activities, and meant that the reminders of the virus, and poor governmental and societal response, are ubiquitous.

We are fortunate that the school district our children attend is large enough to have had the means and organizational capacity to purchase access to an online curriculum. It was chosen to allow flexibility for students and educators to move between online and face-to-face meeting as conditions dictated. Unfortunately, as is often the case with learning software, the limited demand and niche market that spawned the software made it more useful for families where an adult could accompany the student when completing the lessons, or at the very least, was much better suited to a child who is old enough to read independently. The result is that the third grade teachers have adapted their online instruction to sidestep the awkward interface, while the third graders themselves have learned to navigate it. However, our first grader has neither the computer experience, nor the patience to try to navigate this wonky interface, and they now associated independent learning activities with the frustrations of this platform.

Social isolation has been the most taxing. We live in a place where the public policy response has been muted, and compliance lax relative to some of the areas that were hardest hit in the early days of the pandemic. Even in a city where there has been more focus by the local government on limiting spread, the tensions between economic and health policy have been strong. Response in the community has mirrored this tension. As a result, it has been difficult to know who we think our kids could safely play with under circumstances all would find acceptable. Some families don't want to wear masks (okay, none of us wants to wear them, but some are more resistant than others to actually doing it), others don't want to interact with anyone outside of who they have decided to include in a pod.

For months we didn't see our kid's friends in any in-person setting, and the toll that took on them was very quickly evident. We were all less patient, faster to outwardly express frustration, and slower to realize what element of pandemic life was causing that frustration. One morning in the spring we found our 6-year-old hiding in his closet. Since that point, maintaining social-emotional health has taken highest priority. Since we live in a city, we are reliant on shared public spaces. In the early months of the pandemic, there was no enforcement of social distancing, nor mask mandates where we lived. So, even as we tried to go to a park to get some change from our house environment (which we are fortunate to have), we could not enjoy the park when most people around us were not wearing a mask or attempting to social distance.

Our 8-year-old has been able to maintain a few friendships and interactions via video chat. This is in part because we have friends who are strictly self-isolating because of their own health needs, and so the video connection was mutually beneficial for our children. There has not been an analogous connection for our 6-year-old, however, and so it has been harder on him. Though we do not go out in public otherwise, we did make several road trips to see family. Our zero interactions with people while home meant the only risk of exposure was in gas stations (no hotel stays were needed), since we also pre-packed all of our own food and drinks. These few family visits became our sanity. Both the act of visiting other spaces and people, but also looking forward to them. As winter has descended, we are grateful to live in a place where the weather is milder and outdoor activities can still be comfortably enjoyed. Yet, post-Thanksgiving spikes have made it less appealing to venture out, and schools that had been open for two months are again closed. The good news is that the schools demonstrated they were places of zero spread, even as the city cases spiked. So, there is hope for spring that schools might safely reopen and our kids get back to something closer to normal. In the meantime, we will steel ourselves against the urge to get too adventurous as this is now the most dangerous period of spread yet. Although, after testing negative for the virus we made one more road trip to visit family that are self-quarantined. Of course, nothing carries zero risk, but we've all had to make choices about what risks we could take on, and since school exposure was not an option for us, we have tried to take one form of isolation as an opportunity to reduce another.

As the year has progressed, we are even more aware how privileged we are to have two adults in our home, both of whom can do their jobs remotely. Job loss was not a risk, but health concerns, and a community context where we had limited trust that either schools or babysitters could be safely engaged, meant that we have kept to ourselves more than maybe is advisable. A few families have opened up to outside play while wearing masks, and that has helped. One of the hardest parts about parenting, in general, is not knowing how much of the uncertainty of life to convey to your children. A global pandemic has heightened that to a degree that I could never have imagined.

CHAPTER 16

WHEN GOING AWAY TO SCHOOL GOES AWAY

Sarah L. Woulfin

Every morning we wait for the school bus at the bottom of the driveway. Sometimes we pretend to be animals: T, a tiger, and me, a flamingo. Sometimes we count by 2s, or 5s, or 10s. Sometimes we run laps up and down the driveway or try yoga poses. Sometimes we step on the large rocks in the yard as if conquering a realm. Then the bus crests over the hill, slows down while approaching our driveway, and stops. I double check T's backpack, give him a hug, encourage him to have a great day at school, and remind him that he'll come back home in the afternoon. Next, and perhaps most importantly, we do meow-meow, our handshake, with one hand, or tiger paw, fitting into another, arcing up and down as we say "meow-meow" in unison. That is how T says bye before his giant steps at school; that is how I say I love you to my tiger, an autistic 7-year-old.

After March 13, the COVID-19 school closures removed this routine, pausing our meow-meow ritual. During the spring, we weren't saying bye, he wasn't getting on the bus, and he wasn't having a day with adventures in his world: an amazing elementary school. Without this routine and his venture to a different place—an inclusive school building with caring adults, wonderful supports, and classmates—home and school were smooshed into

Parenting in the Pandemic: The Collision of School, Work, and Life at Home, pp. 77–79
Copyright © 2021 by Information Age Publishing

the same space. My tiger stayed home for remote learning, and we missed the place and space of school.

It is deeply taken for granted that elementary school-aged children will learn reading, writing, math, and also social-emotional skills at school. Many children do continue developing those skills at home via remote learning, but for autistic children, like T, there are obstacles when schooling enters the home, and there are deep losses of the place and space of school.

As a mom, advocate for public schools and social justice, and education policy researcher, I learned much about remote learning and the nuances of special education from the shocks of the pandemic. So, I could share how we instituted Tiger School with a brightly colored poster and rewards (LEGO sets, of course!). I could share the strategies I dug up from my own teaching experience in California in the early 2000s. I could share successes with literacy and math activities as well as a handful of challenges, from a jumpy dog to a loud song in an instructional video. Instead, I will share my realizations about what the place and space of school was teaching T. I learned that although T was gaining knowledge and skills for reading, writing, and math away at school, he had also been learning in and through our driveway time, his bus ride, the experience of going away to school, trying new activities and engaging with multiple adults and children, and the routine of coming back home to our family.

My tiger learned on the bus. T could find a seat, talk with other kids, and even share a book with them. T enjoyed bringing his Pokemon handbook to show other kids or to review on his own. These conversations and time with text mattered for building confidence, forming friendships, and developing literacy skills.

At school, T was learning inside and outside the classroom. He was practicing putting away items, using his locker, zipping his jacket. He was making decisions about what to eat for lunch, such as whether to grab chocolate milk, and eagerly enjoying the #1 favorite school lunch of chicken and waffles. He was waiting in line at lunch, but also in physical education or to check-out a library book. More importantly, he was seeing and conversing with adults, from the art teacher and school psychologist to the school cafeteria workers and principal. Of course, he was engaging with and learning from his stellar first grade teacher, choosing books for his book box, writing pieces in his workshop folder, drawing Minecraft characters, and playing math games.

I'll pause to state that T is fully included at school. And I'll pronounce that 'treating' or 'fixing' autism via interventions, or an array of services, is *not* our approach. We support and encourage T to be his own tiger, celebrating his milestones and understanding his worries. This includes giving kudos for finding (and wearing) a hat and gloves in winter and inventing tactics for eating pancakes with syrup without getting sticky hands. Grounded in understanding, we do these things for comfort in our home and for our family.

But now I see that the intervention, the substantive support for T, is in actuality the place and space of school. For T's development, sensory processing, and anxiety, the solution is not a policy, program, practice, or even person. Instead, the solution is constituted by the routines, interactions, environment, and communities of school. It is the place of school that makes a difference, strengthening strategies, boosting confidence, and nurturing his stripes. It is the space of school that opens windows for T, enabling him to enter other places. The integration of an autistic child into the place of school matters, so providing the space for an autistic child to grow (and even roar) matters before, during, and after the pandemic.

CHAPTER 17

SHOULD THE KIDS GO BACK TO SCHOOL?

Wrong Answers Only

Erin Marie Furtak

This difficult decision of how kids should return to school in so many places has played out like this. The federal government left it to the states, the states left it to the schools, and the schools left it to the parents. And how are the parents supposed to know what the right answer is to any of this?

—Stephanie Wang, *This American Life* (The Long-Awaited Asteroid Hits Earth),

My kids were 6 and 9 in early March when the pandemic hit. I had already taken two out-of-state trips that month, was furiously completing manuscripts for two spring conferences, revising a book proposal, teaching a doctoral research methods course, reviewing fall instructor appointments, advising two students completing dissertations, running a research-practice partnership with a local school district, and facilitating a pre-tenure faculty mentoring program. In short, living my regular life as a professor and associate dean.

When my kids' school shut down, my husband and I—like so many other working parents—suddenly had to juggle our own complex sched-

Parenting in the Pandemic: The Collision of School, Work, and Life at Home, pp. 81–84
Copyright © 2021 by Information Age Publishing

ules with supporting our kids through remote learning. We were fortunate to both work from home, but our jobs—my husband works for a local non-profit—exploded with new meetings and tasks as our organizations pivoted overnight to adapt to working from home. Somehow, we managed for months without in-person help. My husband and I took turns supervising the kids through the day to make space for our own meetings. Grandparents read stories on FaceTime each day just so we could have a break.

I empathized with my kids' teachers, who were asked to migrate their curricula online over a three-day weekend. At the same time, I struggled to motivate my children and keep my cool as I tried to support them through a long list of tasks each day. As far as I could tell, new learning stopped the day the school closed, with the remaining weeks of the semester consisting of endless worksheets uploaded to Seesaw, math review sheets, and YouTube videos. As an online commentator described, it was like school had been pushed through a sieve, with only the uninteresting, busywork passing through. The teachers tried their best to engage the kids, holding live lessons each day to connect with their students—but trying to track my own meetings alongside my kids' shifting schedules sent me into cognitive overload.

My scholarship unquestionably suffered. A paper I submitted during that time was rejected, with a reviewer noting, "I realize we are all working in COVID—hard time for a manuscript." I was incensed, but then saw the line to which the reviewer was reacting, in my submitted paper:

This paper examines an effort to engage high school biology teachers in shifting their classroom practices from XXX to XXX through the collaborative design of curriculum-embedded formative assessment tasks.

Yeah, I had left that in.

Send Them Back?

As we muddled through the spring, our local school district—unabashedly optimistic, and seemingly apropos of any epidemiological information—declared they would return to 100% in-person instruction in the fall with a 100% remote option. Parents could decide. Almost reflexively, we planned to send our kids back. Surely the pandemic would subside over the summer, and by fall infection rates would be low enough that school would be safe. As a former classroom teacher, I also thought—naively, in retrospect—that in-person learning would better support our local school and teachers.

While we were in isolation, though, our neighbors were talking. They invited us more than once to enjoy beers and wine slushies on a warm summer evening while their children roamed and mixed freely. Keeping to public health guidance, we always declined. Later, I realized, they were discussing choices about school. Was that casual 'what are you doing next fall?' an invitation to join a learning pod? While I bought my kids new backpacks, ordered masks, and pondered after-school decontamination routines, infection trends were heading in the wrong direction. It seemed inevitable that it would not be safe for teachers and students to gather in school anytime soon.

I now realize I was waiting for someone in power to decide to close schools again —but by early August, there was still no direction from the top. The President's unambiguous "LIBERATE" tweets translated through the Department of Education into pressure to open the schools. Suddenly, our family's decision aligned with White House policy. In contrast, my friends in Singapore and Germany had kids back in school for a long time. The difference, I came to realize, was strong, centralized guidance: more intense lockdowns, government-distributed PPE, and well-organized contact tracing. But in the U.S.? Just reopen. Temperature checks, but no PPE. BYO masks. Got it, parents? You decide.

My anxiety peaked as the first day of school drew near. As a scholar committed to justice and equity, I carried the burden of our decision acutely. Were we doing the right thing? Supporting our public school was always the best option—right? Wouldn't remote schooling increase educational inequities between families with the resources to support online learning? However, with unions threatening to strike, it was also clear that teachers did not feel safe teaching in person. We were also concerned that the district's plans for reentry would not prevent COVID transmission in the classroom, leading to disruptive shifts from in-person to remote learning. We also worried our kids might become vectors for the virus.

As I grappled with these choices, I slowly learned through text threads and curbside conversations that most of the families in our neighborhood had opted for remote learning. The tables had turned. While we were in isolation, waiting for infection rates to drop to a level that would allow in-person learning, they had acted as though nothing had changed. Now with school starting up again, they would be going into isolation and learning online. At the same time, I had waited for guidance from a system that instead forced individual families to make their own decisions, and was caught back-footed despite months of pondering the "right" choice. As a parent, I felt like a failure.

Wrong Answers Only

After the decision was pushed from the President to the Department of Education to states and districts, the decision ultimately came down to my family and our local school. While other principals in the same district allowed parents to make decisions until the last minute, our interim prin-cipal—who didn't know my kids or my family—enforced a decision date, and the tardiness of our choice meant we were forced to send our kids in-person, or not at all. So in order keep our family safe, to avoid unpredict-able school openings and closures, and to support the teachers, we decided days before school was set to begin to withdraw our kids and enroll them an online charter school.

To make it all work, we merged households with my parents, retired edu-cators and could help us each day. To protect my parents' health, we would continue to isolate. While it gives me joy to see my children and parents together each day, I mourn the loss of our community public school. Are we really supporting teachers by taking our tax dollars to a charter? Will my children be further advantaged when this is all over because of my family's time and resources? There was and still is no clear path that clearly served the way of justice and equity that I seek as a scholar. I've had to accept that the moral clarity I seek may never arrive, and as we eke our way through this school year, I worry daily about my role in exacerbating educational inequities and undermining public school systems.

All the decisions were left to individual parents, among a universe of what felt like bad choices. Learn in-person, put the teachers at risk. Learn remotely, and contribute to opportunity gaps (Figure 17.1).

So what's the right way?

Wrong answers only.

Figure 17.1

Just Let Me Finish This by Maia Suss (age 9)

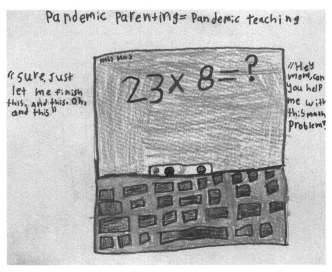

CHAPTER 18

WRESTLING WITH GRACE

Noreen Naseem Rodríguez

In one of two states nationwide without a mask mandate and in a town that was about to welcome 25,000+ students back to campus, I did not feel comfortable sending my children to school in person in the fall. My husband and I opted for online learning without hesitation. After all, my kids were going into second and fifth grades, both of which I taught. I could supplement whatever I needed to!

Turns out, supplementation was not the issue. When I asked my second grader where she wanted to set up her desk, I was flattered when she asked to be in my office. We made room for her desk and dug up frames and a lamp to personalize her space. We hung up a bulletin board and got her a calendar, bringing back pleasant memories of my elementary classroom. Things seemed to be off to a good start.

Then we got her schedule, which revealed that her daily morning meeting coincided with the time I taught online. Her headphones were uncomfortable, so when I wasn't teaching, she preferred to have them off, which meant I listened to every lesson and class meeting for the first several days of school. As a former second grade teacher, listening to her teacher struggle through online learning was excruciating. For the first few weeks of school, students were required to be on mute unless they were directly called on; these 7- and 8-year-old children, many of whom had not interacted with

Parenting in the Pandemic: The Collision of School, Work, and Life at Home, pp. 85–88
Copyright © 2021 by Information Age Publishing
85

their peers since in-person schooling ended in mid-March, were *desperate* to talk to their friends and peers. And this teacher refused to offer them opportunities to do this.

My fifth grader's teacher, on the other hand, was the epitome of what you would want for a first online learning experience. She was warm and created functional yet aesthetically pleasing online materials. She provided instructional videos so students could see how to use new apps and functions, and opened each day with morning meetings filled with group games and jokes. It was impossible for me to not compare the two.

At the same time, I knew this wasn't easy for anyone. I was still in close contact with a friend from my teaching days. In those early weeks of the fall semester, she shared her makeshift document camera set-up and materials with me, making clear how sharp the learning curve was even for experienced teachers. Therefore, I hesitated to say anything to my daughter's second grade teacher. She was new to the online platform and had yet to build a significant relationship with my daughter or our family. Was it fair for me to criticize her during a global pandemic, at the start of a school year that no one could have possibly anticipated? Of course not.

So I held my tongue. I tried to give her grace, just as I hoped my undergraduate students would grant me as I taught online while unexpectedly providing constant support to my own children. But not only am I a former teacher, I am a social studies teacher educator. In my professional capacity, I conduct professional development at the state and local level. Throughout the day, I overheard class meetings and the instructions for assignments. While I could be intentional about not critiquing struggles related to the online platform, I could not stay silent about terrible pedagogy out of alignment with state standards.

Here's the thing–in January, my colleague and I were asked by the local district to do a workshop to support teachers in implementing the new state standards in social studies. Because I teach elementary social studies methods, I know those grade level standards particularly well. So imagine my surprise when I heard my daughter's teacher announce that the week's social studies learning would be focused on days of the week and months of the year. Calendars are *not* a part of social studies standards. Some might argue that calendar learning fits best in math (as part of the development of numerical fluency) or as part of the daily routine. But nowhere, not even in kindergarten, are these ideas part of elementary social studies curriculum.

Long story short, I contacted the principal as well as the district's curriculum supervisors who had invited me and my colleague to do the workshop the previous year. The principal spoke to the teacher, who was using the district's previous social studies curriculum; apparently the transition to current educational standards did not happen due to COVID. Once I learned that, my issue was no longer with the teacher but with the district, which was allowing inappropriate content to be passed off as on-level learning. Two months later, I can't say that I've been pleased with this teacher's curricular content choices, but I am choosing to leave her be. She has offered more opportunities for students to engage in open conversation, increased the number of synchronous meetings, and is clearly trying to do better. In many ways, this academic semester is a wash. While I think it is within my rights as a parent to demand that the district maintain standards of curricular rigor, I don't think the teacher needs any extra demands on her individual plate. Moreover, I'm able to support and be present for my kids in ways that many parents are not able. This privilege is what keeps me from burdening others.

Parenting during a pandemic has tested many of us. I am going up for tenure next year and I am in the middle of writing a book. I did not anticipate completing these major professional landmarks while supporting my children with their schooling during the traditional school day with zero childcare support. I'm certain none of us wanted things to be this way, so I have to give myself some grace. I'm doing the best that I can with what I've been given, and I have to assume others are, too (see Figure 18.1 and 18.2).

Figure 18.1

Untitled 1 by Lucia age 10)

Figure 18.2

Untitled 2 by Lucia (age 10)

CHAPTER 19

PARADOXES, PEDAGOGY, AND PARENTING

Patrick Proctor

I was raised by educators. My mother was a special education teacher and a reading specialist. My father was a superintendent. My parents believed (and still believe) strongly in public education and the promise it holds as one of the only U.S. institutions that must allow everyone to attend no matter what. As an education professor who works with teachers and in schools, I hold on to these views. My work focuses on language development, literacy, and bilingualism. I have been trained as a classroom observer and as an applied linguist. I am good at hanging out in classrooms, making connections with students and their teachers, and at analyzing lots of types of language data. But there was no preparation that I, or any of us, could have received, no environment that could have oriented us, to deal with a global pandemic that pushed schools into either going remote, or into face-to-face instruction that required educators to turn their backs on group work, discourse, and other practices that we know promote learning in school. But my own experience with the pandemic, as an educator and as a parent, required that I get back to the essence, and directly engage some of the basic human needs that support learning in school.

Parenting in the Pandemic: The Collision of School, Work, and Life at Home, pp. 89–92
Copyright © 2021 by Information Age Publishing
89

When the pandemic hit, and school went fully remote, my daughter was in seventh grade. She's a smart, shy, and empathic person. She prefers the company of a couple excellent friends over a gaggle of acquaintances who only superficially know each other. During her first two years of middle school, she struggled with the social pressures that accompany the age. At school, she would sometimes be left out of small group discussions, lunch gatherings, or big roles in school musicals. At least two times a week, getting her out of bed, dressed and fed, and off to school was difficult, to say the least. She did well in her classes, and found some teachers more engaging than others. Rarely did she have the energy or the interest to explain why or how some teachers were better for her than others. For my part, "back to school" nights were tedious and uninformative, except to finally get to put a teacher's face to a name, and listen to a generic report—out to the group of parents that was able to show up that particular evening. It was not ideal. It was not terrible. It was typical middle school life in a privileged, predominantly white community here in the Northeastern United States.

Then the pandemic hit, and for all of us, things changed. Amidst the fear, confusion, and sadness, my daughter's school went entirely online. There was an adjustment period as administrators, teachers, students, and caregivers tried to figure things out. Our household was and is fortunate. My wife and I have jobs that easily moved to online spaces, making it possible for us to support our daughter. While my wife's 9–5 work did not stop, my work hours were more flexible, and so I took on three major roles during this time that have since influenced my perspective on teaching and learning.

First, in our home, I am the cafeteria manager. I am in charge of making sure the kitchen stays clean and that breakfasts and lunches are accessible and ready. This simulates a school situation in which students do not have to worry about where their next meal is coming from, which sets up a foundation for learning. Engaging in this kind of daily preparation and clean up made me realize how fortunate our family has been in terms of having access to food and nutrition. It decentered me from my daily work pressures, and made me practically understand the enduring Maslow's hierarchy of needs (see Figure 19.1), which suggests that, at base level, humans have physiological needs that, if not met, keep us from meeting our psychological and self-fulfillment needs. As an educator, I felt repurposed through food preparation, and gained new respect for those in our schools who dedicate themselves to feeding the children who attend them.

My second role was gym teacher. As most anyone acquainted now with online school, physical education is very difficult. Short of doing jumping jacks or stretches in front of a computer screen, or being told by the teacher to go walk around the block and come back, teaching physical education is a challenging task. When the pandemic hit, it was springtime, and this

Figure 19.1

Maslow's Hierarchy of Needs

presented a second opportunity to attend to physiological needs by getting my daughter outside. During this time, we bubbled with our upstairs neighbor and her fifth grade daughter who joined our activities. I planned hikes, and taught my two students how to play corn hole, croquet, and other lawn games. When we first started hiking, the girls were in terrible shape. A 1-mile hike on level ground resulted in multiple complaints of sore legs, tired lungs, and burning thirst. But we persisted, every Wednesday for two months, until by the end, our summative assessment was a 2-mile hike to the summit of a nearby mountain. While there were still complaints, they did it. Targeting food and exercise during the pandemic gave me renewed respect for these physiological needs and the efforts of our cafeteria workers and physical education teachers.

Finally, during this time, I returned to my roots as a classroom observer. For some reason, my daughter early on decided that she did not want to do her classes in her room, but preferred instead to be in the dining room of our apartment. She didn't use headphones. So, while prepping lunch, or doing my own work, I was able to observe much of the instruction she received in online school. I listened and watched (when her camera was off) as her science, math, English, Mandarin, and social studies teachers ran their online classrooms. I noted whether and how they did group-work (often painful in zoom), if they lectured or cold-called students, and explored the different tools they used to engage their students. It was better than attending back to school night. As her teachers worked to do something that had never been done before, and amidst the fear of the pandemic, my daughter actually started to like it. She remarked at the peace that came from not having to deal with the social pressures of going into school. She liked the increase in independent work, and opportunities to check in with her teachers. She felt calmer, which, along with lunch and gym time, allowed us to think and talk more about the psychological needs she was feeling regarding friendships, school aptitudes, and her interactions with her family.

During this time, I have also been working closely with practicing bilingual teachers in school districts, who serve students across grade levels who are at various stages of language development, and who sometimes present with more physiological and safety needs than in my family. These experiences with my bilingual teacher colleagues helped me make better sense of my home-based observations. Like my daughter's teachers, these educators work tirelessly to meet their students' needs and confirm my observations that there exist many challenges to translation software, to providing visuals and videos that support instruction, and to creating safe spaces through zoom where students can talk to their teachers and with each other about the content of their classes. Alongside the challenges, however, teachers note feeling closer to students in their homes. Parents are sometimes online with their children, and they report being able to more quickly engage parents that have in the past proven difficult to reach. As a group, we identified early on that we also now have to think about "free and reduced price internet" as much as free and reduced price meals, which adds burden to vulnerable children and their families at the base of Maslow's hierarchy.

Across the time that we spent (and are spending) at home, away from friends, loved ones, and colleagues, I have felt the pain, relief, sadness, and joy that comes with recognizing and attending to our basic human needs. I have witnessed teachers working tirelessly to engage their students in settings that are not particularly conducive to engagement. In general, I am not sure what lessons I have learned from all this yet. We're still in it. I guess so far the main takeaway for me is that we share a common humanity—anyone can contract this virus—and we are dependent on those basic human needs. But the pandemic has made it abundantly clear that some are more likely than to suffer than others, and this suffering is frequently stratified by race, class, age, and ability status. Alongside this, I've also witnessed how teachers are able to recognize these realities more clearly than most anyone. Their efforts combat them through zoom portals, masks, and face shields show love and dedication to the craft that will help us all get through.

CHAPTER 20

A PROCESS OF LIVING

Rebecca Lowenhaupt

"I hate school," Ella sighs as she opens up her laptop and settles into her first class of the morning. It is mid-April about a month into the pandemic, and I don't know whether to count myself lucky or burst into tears at this first time I have ever heard either of my children say that about their beloved school. Ever since they were each in preschool, they have attended the small, progressive private school where our family life has been centered for nearly 10 years. And where we always look forward to seeing our friends, teachers, and other parents in the hallways, library, playground, and the bench in front of the school where those of us with flexible schedules linger and chat in the mornings before heading off to our various obligations. Of course, the bench and other shared spaces where I got to participate in my children's education and community are now suddenly and explicitly off-limits to us all. I'm not surprised. This pandemic is full of firsts, first homemade mask, first friends with COVID, first quarantine birthdays, first Netflix parties, and now this. The first time I've had to advise my child to adjust expectations, go through the motions, simply endure school and wait for time to pass.

I teach John Dewey's *Pedagogic Creed* each semester, an educational philosophy written in the 1890s that serves as a foundation for many progressive education movements even today. Each time we read it, I have

Parenting in the Pandemic: The Collision of School, Work, and Life at Home, pp. 93–95
Copyright © 2021 by Information Age Publishing

reflected on how fortunate my family is to be part of a progressive school that embraces the social dimensions of learning alongside the academic and helps students "use their power for social ends." In the midst of the closure, with all of us isolated, the school's efforts to move online are framed by this value. In a community meeting, the principal talks about our commitment to do this tough thing in community as a way to contribute to the common good, a form of justice we can enact from the comfort of our own homes. Hanna has math conversations with teachers and friends on Zoom, and Ella's advisory continues to meet online each morning. Everyone is trying, but ultimately this is not what any of us want school to be.

As we discuss Dewey this semester, I get stuck on his statement, "I believe that education, therefore, is a process of living and not a preparation for future living." But what would he say about education in a pandemic? What if school is happening at the kitchen table and our current process of living involves unfettered screen time and endless worry? What if all we desperately want is to move beyond this time and into the future? Preparing for the future doesn't seem like such a bad idea when this is our present.

Over the course of these months, I have often wondered how to reclaim this time as we engage in this process of living. "Time is stretching and shrinking," a friend texts. The days are short, the weeks are long, and I'm having trouble holding onto it. But I try. Tinkering with the schedule, holding tight to routine, ending the day with reflection and escape. The first several weeks, I diligently write out our schedule in the morning, and revise it in the evening. We make a plan, we set goals, we check in about our progress. These are all the motions of school, but now they are happening at home. On the weekends, it is both a comfort and unmooring that there is no schedule to frame our days. Approximating school gives us a sense of normalcy and helps anchor us. We try to find ways to note the passage of time and create ritual in routine. Even so, often whole days will slip by without any sense of how we spent the hours. Each day, I write in my journal and note the number of days that have passed, but it feels unfathomable as I watch the numbers grow larger, first double digits, then triple. I'm not the only one trying to mark time. Ella has committed to drawing each day, portraits of strangers found online. She signs and numbers each one, and watches them accumulate as time goes by. I remember the 100th day of school celebration, a tradition in so many classrooms, which always seemed odd to me, and think I understand it now, as we cross into triple digits on our count of days at home. Dewey envisioned that, "school life should grow gradually out of the home life; that it should take up and continue the activities with which the child is already familiar in the home." In the pandemic, we have tried to do just the opposite, framing our time at home through the rhythms and routines of school.

I force reflection on our process of living, although it highlights both the good and bad of our days as we share roses and thorns at dinner. There are the days when Hanna sighs and says, "There were no roses today," but there were also a few rare days when they would say, "There were no thorns today!" Often, our thorns involve missing our old lives, routines, and friends. Our roses center on minor triumphs and accomplishments, finishing an assignment or a delicious recipe. Sometimes, our roses are simply getting through another day with our optimism intact.

The routines of home/school seem to crystallize what matters most, and also highlight the stark difference between our plodding days at home and the vibrant, creative community at school. At times, I manage to hold the two at once, the peaceful productivity we have achieved for a few precarious moments and the immense, growing sense of loss that saturates our world right now. At one point, Ella wonders aloud, "Do you think we will look back on this time one day and say, 'Remember what a strange time that was!?' Or instead, will we look back on this time and say, 'Remember how different our life was before?'" And nearly six months later, Hanna asks, "Mom, what if this is normal now, and we never go back?" I really don't know how to answer. I drive by the school and wonder when we will be there again for a regular school day. Until then, we are approximating school at home, trying to find ways to shape our "process of living," while also preparing for an uncertain future.

REFERENCE

Dewey, J. (1897). *My pedagogic creed* (No. 25). EL Kellogg & Company.

CHAPTER 21

WE ARE SENSITIZED
TO RARENESS

William R. Black

I live in Tampa, Florida in a three-generation household-my wife Jessica
and myself, Jessica's parents, and our two children Gabriel (16), and David
(9). We frequently visit my mother, who in her early 80s and lives alone.
And, we have a puppy companion who joined the household just before
the pandemic hit: Jelly the Labradoodle. Our home, my mom's home, and
neighborhood outdoor spaces have constituted our physical world since
early March of 2020. There have been no visits to neighbors or friends'
houses. No socially distant happy hours or dinners. No babysitters and no
caretakers for Gabriel, no education pods or play dates for David. While it
was clear to me early in the "Coronavirus Time" (as my son David calls it)
that the pandemic would continue for a while—despite our earnest desire
to return to our cotidian processes, the decision to physically isolate has
unfortunately been supported over the last 10 months as I accumulated
a stream of memories of COVID-related deaths of colleagues, former students, and relatives of colleagues.

Parenting in the Pandemic: The Collision of School, Work, and Life at Home, pp. 97–101
Copyright © 2021 by Information Age Publishing

On Being Sensitized to Rareness

On May 22 of 2020, Florida Governor DeSantis opened all youth activities to face to face activities-including schools and summer camps. He said confidently that children are not very effective spreaders of the coronavirus. DeSantis' family pediatrician sat beside the governor and said that illness from Covid is "extremely rare" in children and that the anxiety and depression of isolation is more harmful. It is time to let kids be kids she said. I have become sensitized to rareness as a central component of my life with others and as a parent. Gaby is missing the short (p) leg of his 18th chromosome and some transplantation of the long (q) leg and lost verbal language at age 4 and therefore diagnosed with Autism. His chromosomal makeup is not only very rare, but also central to who he is—and by extension, who we are. Our living arrangement that includes five people who are high risk is also uncommon—and a bit rare amongst my colleagues. The image of Gaby, who is high-risk, by himself in a hospital with no ability to communicate verbally (autism and 18 p– syndrome); relatives on ventilators, and the lack of trust in federal responses and state government approaches in Florida have led us to construct a year of careful protections.

On the very same day the governor spoke (May 22) Patricia Ripley threw her 9-year-old autistic son into a canal and intentionally drowned him in Miami. The very stress of caring for the son contributed to her mental health issues. On May 26, I saw the video of her drowning her son on Univision in Miami. I felt very hesitant to see the video, but found that I could not look away. The video literally took my breath away. I knew exactly where this awful event happened—about a mile from my in-laws former home in Miami. I saw her walk with her son—who walked and looked like Gaby—and push him into the water in a spot on the edge of a golf course and park I had been by many times before-sometimes with Gaby in a stroller. I could not sleep. Jessica and I talked about how horrible it was, but not without recognizing stress and some iota of sympathy for the situation.

Early in the week Patricia Ripley had tried to avoid responsibility by falsely reporting that her son was abducted by a Black man with a gun. On May 25, George Floyd was murdered by police—the latest and not the last in a string of anti-Blackness brutality. As a professor we were called upon to respond. I was also in charge of helping to plan the UCEA convention and we had to also make the call to pivot from San Juan to an online convention. The racial and COVID pandemics roared through the summer and I felt conflicted and powerless at times. My general optimism was too often replaced with stewing over how people don't care about others. Throughout this year, I at times felt quite frustrated, angry, and less than what I want to be. I felt I needed to do more—I should be called to do more-and I was not doing anything well.

Tracks and Tribulations: Schooling in a Pandemic

After what seemed to be weekly and then monthly updates on potential school reopenings in the spring semester, David's third grade school year was finally finished online. David's teachers generally navigated the online environment with competency, courage, and commitment to success. In general, we did not feel that he lost that much instruction and we were comfortable with online schooling in the fall.

As we prepared to return to school in the fall, David's fourth grade teachers reached out to him and held multiple orientations the two weeks before school. He was able to get the same great teacher he had in second grade for language arts and social studies, and then had two gifted teachers who sent very detailed instructions to the 15 students in their charge. The effort and organization of the school has been good in spite of the challenges. While the accumulation of time online and continued challenges of our space have led him to be "tired," in general he has continued to learn with a wonderful and committed set of teachers. The greater challenges have begun to be around activity and motivation to go do activities outside.

In contrast to his experience, institutional divergences and marginalizations have literally been brought home during the pandemic. Back in the spring, Gaby was attending a school run by applied behavior analysis (ABA) therapists—it was expensive and not particularly effective—but was safe and he had a one-to-one aide, which was paid for by insurance and a voucher. During middle school, we had been trying alternative approaches. As he had only a few months left before he aged out of middle school, and it was a year-round school, we kept him enrolled in the school during the spring. However, it was soon clear that there would be little contact between the "teacher" (noncredentialed) who barely reached out to us. When she did, she literally asked us what we were doing so she could put it in her report in order that the school get voucher money. As there was little happening educationally, we clearly saw limits of voucher system accountability and refused to sign the check for the voucher. It seemed completely unethical—and we did not want to bill insurance for ABA therapy that was online and ineffective. We were the ones having to do the work and they were billing. To make the weird even stranger—we had an Individualized Educational Plan (IEP) online for the fall admission to the high school. In order to hold the IEP meeting per district protocols, he needed to be in the system—so he was enrolled in a middle school in April on paper, but he did not attend. His ABA school had reopened—and immediately reopened with a therapist who tested positive, so that was never an option for us.

Consider the excitement of your child starting high school as a ninth grader. After multiple phone calls and e-mails, we got to the weekend before school started with no information about his teacher was or how to access school material online. We got a phone call the Sunday before class was to begin from this primary teacher. Despite Gaby and students in the exceptional student education (ESE) segregated classroom all "bringing" higher levels of funding to the school, Gaby's teacher started the year with a student enrollment of 35 kids. Gaby has class with his teacher for one hour and 15 minutes every day, while David has class from 7:40–2:00. Jessica and I try not to interfere with Gaby's class, but we need to provide complete support for him to engage for the 1 hour (and then 15 minutes one on one in the afternoon) so we are present. We try to stay in the background in order to respect the teaching spaces that we now inhabit.

Gaby has intermittent speech therapy at school that is not worth attending. He started the year with math and science teacher in the afternoon who would constantly be pulled for other duties and would not plan for class (again recognizing the charade that some online learning can be for people like Gaby). It got to the point that I just said that Gaby will not be attending school in the afternoon—it was not appropriate. Yet, his morning teacher is dedicated and has found a way to connect with Gaby. The institution we call school—we are not so sure it is that for Gaby. So, during the last 10 months we rotate supports with Jessica, myself, and his grandparents during the day—as there are no other supports. More time in school, means more work from us-and where might that extra time come from? So, we have reached a totally unsatisfactory compromise of sorts. My frustration, anger, and sadness—as well as patience have all been felt very often.

Sliver by the River

Given these dynamics, I began a new ritual of taking Gaby for a walk most days of the week at a park at the very end of our neighborhood. The park is far removed from any major streets and has very few visitors—it is a space I feel safe walking around without a mask. River Park is a sliver with walking trails and a soft sandy road that leads to a small dock on the upper Hillsborough River. The river eventually flows through downtown Tampa into Tampa Bay 15 winding miles later. The park resembles "old" Florida with oaks, palmetto palms, River Cypress, various wading birds, armadillos, Spanish Moss, and of course alligators, snakes, turtles, and mosquitos. We would often go in the morning at eight with golden hue coming through the Spanish Moss. In the spring, we saw the water recede with drier conditions and alligators swim slowly across the river—with an occasional bull gator growl. Gaby began to pick out a favorite path of about a mile in length that takes us through the sandy road and smaller pathways. In so many ways this seemed like more of a meaningful activity than forced ABA repetitions—what we had called school. As the summer came, the cricket and frog colonies come out for a couple of weeks at a time—and mosquito spray was used liberally. While we walk or drive to and from the park, I can call and catch up with my co-instructors and plan for class or call program advisors around program decisions—the drive is part of my work space.

As Gaby and I end the year in the "winter" with our hikes at River Park, the sun is lays lower in the horizon and we finally are able to enjoy days without heat. The alligators are becoming easier to spot again. The sand-hill cranes still sing their "scraw-scraw" as they fly by and Gaby still points to the occasional airplane engine humming in the sky above us. We look out for gators swimming in the river and snakes traveling across the road. We listen for the red-crested woodpecker tapping, tapping on a tree. We look at the light in the trees reflecting across the water at different angles now than at the beginning of the pandemic. Gaby will occasionally run—and take his seat on his favorite resting spot—a lichen colored fallen palm tree. Then we get up and continue our walk and I try to remember to be present as this is our school, and this is our time that we will never get back. On Monday, December 14, the initial Pfizer vaccine is given at Tampa General Hospital at the desembarkment of the same river Gaby and I visit that day. Walking down the paths and sandy road through all the trees, water, wildlife in the relative isolation of the park, I am hopeful, but already feeling nostalgia for the time that we have spent at River Park during the pandemic year. I am sensitized to the rareness of our constrained and beautiful journeys together on this slim sliver of parkland by the river.

Figure 21.1

Gaby and his Dad in the Park

CHAPTER 22

THE ONLY WAY IS THROUGH

Parenting My Teenagers
in a World Upended

Sharon Radd

In the fall of 2019, a series of seemingly unrelated health issues dating back to 2017 culminated—quite surprisingly—in the need for me to undergo open-heart surgery at the end of September. I spent the entire 2019 fall semester preparing to go on medical leave, then having surgery, then slowly recovering and eventually working part-time from home. When I went back to work on campus on January 6, 2020, news of a highly contagious and sometimes deadly virus emerging on the other side of the world had just begun to whisper to us here in the United States.

When I left my office on Thursday, March 12th—less than 10 weeks since I'd returned from my medical leave and before my campus had actually shut down—I planned to stay home for the next two weeks. I made this decision based upon my compromised immunity and my still-recovering heart and cardiovascular system. I didn't mind this personal "shut down" one bit: I'm introverted by nature, and I had become ill three times in the 10 weeks I'd

Parenting in the Pandemic: The Collision of School, Work, and Life at Home, pp. 103–105

been back at work. I thought a little more time to cocoon and sleep, and less time commuting and getting to meetings, would serve my healing well.

Similarly, the Minneapolis Public Schools—where my husband is a teacher, and my two teenagers attend high school—were making their own plans. They closed on March 17 for at least three weeks; they stayed closed the remainder of the calendar year and will continue well into 2021.

While I was able to deliver a meaningful educational experience to my graduate students the remainder of that semester, my kids' schooling was pretty much a joke. Only it wasn't funny at all. As a junior and a sophomore at the time, and with my husband and I both working, they each had to manage their own school responsibilities. Going to school at the desk in their respective bedrooms often meant clicking into class from their beds, which stretched into spending the entire day and evening in their bedroom. Despite family meals and outdoor activities as a family, they spent the overwhelming majority of hours on their beds. Depression and anxiety lurked at every corner, creeping in like a heavy blanket and taking over too often.

Their schooling last spring made me ask "Why?" Why do they need to go to school now? Why do we continue with this charade as if it is meaningful? What else could we be doing and how else could we be doing it? We all restrict our activity because my underlying health condition puts me at high risk for the most serious—even deadliest—implications of infection. But honestly, even without my heart condition, we would constrain our lives during this pandemic in hopes that we can get through to the other side without any of us dying or having serious long-term health consequences. In what ways is our caution justified, and when is our fear unfounded?

There was—and is—so much to be learned from our current circumstances, yet our systems were clinging to structures, processes and outcomes that kept us locked in a dance to outdated music, unable to hear the new tune, instruments, and arrangements and adjust our movements accordingly. While we've watched our broader society battle over the music we'll play moving forward, within our family we looked for new possibilities, envisioned new options, and watched as my kids became increasingly open to them. My daughter will have taken three college classes by the time she completes high school this spring; my son is taking online saxophone lessons and playing sports in an altered but still rewarding way. They've both taken jobs where they practice work and people skills, all while following stepped-up safety protocols.

School-wise, we rearranged furniture, space, and use-patterns so both kids could attend their online classes sitting at separate desks in the same (not-a-bedroom) room. In many ways, each is the others' classmate, and as a result, their experiences aren't nearly so lonely or isolated. In addition, the school district has structured class time more logically, and their teachers are better equipped in running their classes and assignments, making their time and schooling more valuable. And there is some relief from not being in the "rat race" that is the school year, and the intensity in their over-crowded school.

As has been said *ad nauseum,* this time is unprecedented, globally, nationally, regionally, locally, socially, economically, and politically. In the midst of this turmoil and uncertainty, my kids' lives are radically mutating. At a time when they should be exploring their independence and identities in the world outside of our house—participating in school activities, prioritizing time, and interactions with their peers, exploring our city, testing boundaries, and learning how to manage life beyond these four walls—their world has become persistently quite small. While our creative problem-solving has produced workable and more satisfying solutions, we now know they will have lived in this fundamentally altered way for well over a year before we feel relatively safe venturing out more freely. It's possible my daughter, now a senior, may never return to her high school for classes before she doesn't have a graduation ceremony this spring. My son, at 6'4" and not yet fully grown, may not play another full basketball season during his high school career with his dad and I watching from the stands instead of online. I've been struck, time and again, that they have shown the maturity and self-sacrifice to so regularly safeguard my health rather than mindlessly pursue their own interests and needs. It is both beautiful and heartbreaking at the same time.

They will always remember this time—painfully, regretfully, and hopefully with some pride—their not-yet-long lives haven't prepared them to fully grasp that, on the one hand *this too shall pass* and on the other, *things will never be the same.* The only way through this hopefully once-in-a-lifetime situation is through. And, if they and we can get through this with health and well-being, they are equipped to withstand the other difficulties that will inevitably come their way in the future. We continue to practice living with empathy and compassion, to look for the lessons this experience offers us, to search for the ways we can step into a better future, and to value one another with unending love. That is the best we can do, and perhaps the only thing that truly matters.

CHAPTER 23

MY KIDS WILL BE FINE

What About Everybody Else's?

Joanne M. Marshall

COVID-19 has shown the world the cracks that exist in our systems. Most obviously, we've seen that health care is inadequate and available inequitably to people who are poor. Schools tend to be a societal safety net. In Iowa, where the governor has ruled that schools must be in-person at least 50% of the time unless the county hits a 15% positivity rate, school leaders and communities have struggled with whether to stay open or to close. Our family has also struggled with what to do, but I've become more aware that any risks to my children are buffered by our family's resources. And yet despite those resources, they are struggling for the first time with school. I've gotten one small glimpse of what it might be like for them to be marginalized, a new experience for them and for me. Because of their struggles, I've also learned what I knew from research but now have seen personally: how essential a good teacher is.

As I write this in fall of 2020, the COVID-positive rates in our county are 14.7%, close enough to the required 15%, and the school board has voted to move all students fully online for the third time since March of this year. My two teens (ages 14, 16) have been fully online since the spring, a choice

Parenting in the Pandemic: The Collision of School, Work, and Life at Home, pp. 107–110

our family made together. As professor parents, we believe that school is absolutely important for children's academic and social well-being and that it is essential for a democratic society. But we also think we can keep our children, and by extension, us and the rest of our community, safer if they are not sitting in classrooms every day while, you know, breathing.

We've been able to make fully-online education a workable option for our household because professoring allows us to work mostly from home, our children are older, and we can supplement the content they are missing. While my "office" space is next to the kitchen and my growing teens distract me by coming through approximately every half hour to fix and eat yet another peanut butter sandwich (so *many* sandwiches), they are fairly independent and do not require much monitoring, unlike when they were little. We are also able to provide them with endless peanut butter sandwiches without relying on school breakfasts or lunches. We were able to invest in higher-speed Internet so that all four of us can sustain video connections, and to buy or borrow surplus computer monitors from our institution so that each of us could supplement our work or school-issued laptops with a second and larger screen. Content-wise, my spouse supervises our kids' STEM subjects, and I supervise the humanities.

Our jobs and economic stability and expertise set my children up for online school success that I recognize other families do not have. And yet, despite our offering every home advantage, they still struggle more than usual and their schooling this year seems to be subpar.

Our kids are usually quite good at traditional school. They have favorite subjects, and some come more easily than others, but they know how to study and get things done. They're also able-bodied and white and male, so school is structured for their success. Some of their academic struggle now is lack of accountability and organization on their parts, and some of it is their teachers'. It was hard to get into a routine at first. Teen one was moving towards nocturnality in the spring until we all decided that wasn't sustainable and parentally decreed: "You must go to bed by midnight." Some of the struggle is that online learning takes longer. Teen one explains, for example, "Before, if I had a question, I'd stay after class for two minutes and ask it. Now I email it, and wait two hours for Mr. C. to respond, and 50% of the time he never does."

Some of the struggle comes from the quality of teachers' online organization, which varies by teacher. Some teachers forget to cross-list assignments in both Google Classroom and Infinite Campus, so they're counted as missing even though they've been turned in. When the district is in hybrid mode, alternating in-person school days for half the students with online days for the other half, my kids feel forgotten. Teen two explains, "Everyone has their camera off, and Mr. E calls on the same four people all the time because he knows they'll answer." Or, "Ms. T puts us in breakout rooms and tells us to discuss, but no one does. We just wait for twenty minutes and do our own thing until it's over." There's no point in going to this or that class, they say, because there is no interaction, it's recorded, and they can watch it later at double speed, IF they even need to watch it in order to complete the assignment. It is hard for me to argue with their rationale as long as their grades stay up. They need to be in class because … it helps build good study habits for the future? It shows their teachers that they care? I don't really believe it, and neither do they. Some teachers have given up on creating their own content. While I know from my own years of teaching that stealing ideas from other teachers to try on my own leads me to be more creative—I never would have tried FlipGrid otherwise—some teachers take this a little far, and my kids have noticed: "Mr. H is actually using Ms. R's slides; even though it's a totally different subject. He told us to put 'science' in wherever it says 'social studies' and the project would be about the same. He's actually got her jokes and her Bitmojis and her videos still in there. How lazy is that to not even make your own slides?" (Agreed.) My spouse is teaching math in the evenings because our child doesn't understand it and "my teacher isn't teaching it anyway; he just tells us to read the book and do the problems and let him know if we have questions." Math class meets online in person once a week, the teacher asks if there are any questions, everyone says no, and they dismiss after five minutes. "Why don't you ask your question then?" I ask and am told that he doesn't want to be *that kid* who makes everyone stay in class to get his question answered. Plus, Dad is better at explaining anyway.

I listen to these complaints, and as a professional educator they drive me bananas. I can't help wondering how the system could work better. Who's doing online teaching well? I ask my in-house experts. "Mr. L," comes the prompt answer. "He actually teaches. I go to class because I learn something." On further pressing, I learn that Mr. L is doing what I would call a jigsaw and assigning different pairs to complete different parts of the assignment, which creates a note sheet that will help them complete their assessment at the end of the week. He also does regular formative assessment, notices when people are struggling, and extends or modifies the assignments as necessary. There's also a socioemotional component they like. Mr. V, for example, is "pretty good" because he has new ideas and he "shares something about himself, like his mental health this week. He's also really trying to get to know us as people and not just by our writing." As a parent, I like Mr. V because he sends families a weekly e-mail previewing the upcoming week.

My kids will be fine. This year is (I hope) an anomaly. It's given me a closer glimpse of what my kids' school lives could look like if they were regularly out of the mainstream, and a greater sense of the frustration other families must feel All. The. Time. about their kids' schooling. My research and teaching have focused for a while on inclusive schooling and social justice pedagogy for leaders and teachers, but I'm still left with questions. I want to know *why* some teachers are better *right now*, during the pandemic, than others. Are they better during "normal" school also? (I suspect so.) Do they have better training or coaching or resources? Better motivation or support? And how can schools and preparation programs support the ones who are mediocre, if not downright "lazy?" I know I could raise a (gentle) ruckus on behalf of my kid with each teacher, but that does not solve the problems which are underneath. COVID has exposed many societal problems about which I have little expertise, but supporting better teaching is one that I'll keep working on long-term.

CHAPTER 24

THE CHALLENGES OF MUSIC TEACHING AND LEARNING DURING THE PANDEMIC

Elisa Macedo Dekaney

We were returning to Syracuse from the Nassau Aquatic Center in Long Island when we heard the news of a COVID-19 cluster in Nassau County. For the past three years, we have watched our oldest son, a springboard diver and then a high school senior, compete at the New York state meet. This year, however, in that enclosed aquatic center, filled with parents, guardians, grandparents, siblings, athletes and their coaches all breathing each other's air, sitting shoulder to shoulder, we were oblivious to the fact that we were headed to a global pandemic. It was March 1, 2020.

My husband Josh and I teach music at Syracuse University. At that point, the university was making plans to inform all students to take their belongings when they left for spring break. We had hoped it was going to be a temporary situation, but by then, cases in Europe were escalating without control and we all had a feeling that the students' departures were for the remaining of the semester. After spring break, we transitioned into teaching from home. Josh teaches drum set lessons and the house shook all day while he taught his students. At that time, our sons, a 15-year-old

Parenting in the Pandemic: The Collision of School, Work, and Life at Home, pp. 111–115

sophomore and a 17-year-old senior, were still going to school in person, but it was becoming apparent that soon they too would have to move to a remote learning environment.

And so it was, March 16 marked the first COVID-19 case in Onondaga County and all schools went remote. The pandemic had reached our hometown and the remainder of the school year was going to be online. While teaching our college students remotely, we had to support our sons as they transitioned to the virtual learning environment.

For our oldest son, things were already pretty much done. He had already successfully passed all his regents and had only a few classes in his schedule: physical education, band, English, math, and social studies. None of his teachers held synchronous online classes.

Our sophomore, with a full schedule and several honors classes, was swamped with work and numerous synchronous classes. From our perspective, new content was delivered as if there was no tomorrow and homework load seemed disproportionately high compared to the homework for the in-person instruction. You could see he was becoming depressed, isolated from his friends, trying really hard to learn. His teachers also struggled to meaningfully deliver instruction online.

For some teachers, technology was not part of their everyday teaching. It took a while for some of them to set up their Google classroom and develop meaningful interactions with their students. I remember hearing cheers when Mr. O. finally completed the setup of his virtual classroom. There was much jubilation in our house.

K–12 teachers were not alone in their struggle to transition instruction to online mode; college professors faced similar challenges. While I was already pretty familiar with our online teaching platform, Blackboard, the system itself had not been built to deliver synchronous classes. I, too, struggled with technology and with being an effective teacher in a virtual environment. I remember my first synchronous class using Blackboard Collaborate. I did not know Mac users needed to use the Google Chrome platform instead of Safari if they wanted to share their screen. When it was time to watch a YouTube video relevant to our discussion, I put the link in the chat box and asked each student to watch the video individually and then return to Blackboard. Frankly, I was embarrassed by having to do things this way. I was better prepared for the following class and learned a lot about how to engage students virtually. When the university finally acquired an ADA compliant license for Zoom, things got a little easier.

As important as mastering technology is for remote teaching, building community and supporting the students was my priority because we faced unpredicted challenges with the global pandemic. We knew we would not be able to play our instruments or sing effectively in the virtual environment, but for some of my students our synchronous classes were the only time they were able to interact with one another, check in on each other, and maintain a sense of community that was supported and encouraged during our in-person time. I was concerned with the well-being of my students. One of them went back to South Korea and was alone for two weeks in a state-controlled hotel, fulfilling a mandatory quarantine. Often, I had to check on students individually because they seemed withdrawn, depressed, ill, or lonely in our virtual classes. It became clear that the sense of community brought by the ensemble was what they missed the most.

Transitioning to the remote teaching environment was challenging for the arts, particularly music. As a musician and educator preparing music teachers, I have spent many years learning about the importance of music for people, for society, and for our communities. I have researched its function, its appeal, and its effect on who we are. The context for this understanding has always been through in-person interactions. In my experience, participation in music ensembles is primarily about community building, about belonging and finding the common element that unites the group: music. Students in the K–12 setting, college students, and community members join a music ensemble because they want to make music together. They appreciate the collective sound their voices and instruments produce and are rewarded by the overall result of making music together. Traditionally, music educators have always facilitated these music experiences in person.

Performing musicians are trained to learn, rehearse, and perform in person. The ability to perform synchronously, side by side with another musician, is almost impossible to replicate in the virtual environment because technology is still lagging in this area. In the spring of 2020, very few of us were equipped with proper microphones, high speed internet, software, and other items necessary to deliver meaningful instruction online. In K–12 settings, teachers faced similar challenges. Additionally, it exposed the great inequities of our society in terms of access to hardware, software, high speed internet, and adequate physical space at home to engage in appropriate online instruction.

It was in music, of all disciplines, that my sons faced their biggest challenges. They were both enrolled in band and our sophomore was also enrolled in chorus. From the beginning, the two music teachers approached the challenge very differently. While none of the teachers held synchronous classes initially, the choral teacher managed to have materials uploaded to Google classroom and chose a repertoire that needed to be learned. That teacher soon realized that there was a need for synchronous classes even if students were unable to make music as they used to. What the students missed and needed the most was a sense of belonging, being part of a community. With the teacher's assistance, singers managed to learn one or two pieces and record them using a track with instrumental accompaniment.

Each student recorded their own part over the track and the individual performances were collated and edited in a video. In the final product, they were together, in a video. They recognized each other's faces and voices, and they were an ensemble again. This project kept my son engaged and provided some form of music instruction that was in alignment with the expectations of chorus, which is performing together, in community. I admire that teacher and I am grateful for what chorus meant to my son.

In band, no instruction ever happened. Our senior, a percussionist, was not among the most reliable and engaged students, but our sophomore, a French horn player, was. Over the years, his grades in band were in the 98–99 range. He was dedicated, interested, engaged, and had received "perfect scores" in his state festivals. The band teacher held no synchronous classes and only communicated with parents when it was time to return instruments to school or to submit photos for the senior tribute.

I was constantly asking our sons what kinds of assignments they needed to complete to be successful in band. According to them, they needed to record four playing videos of excerpts submitted by their teacher. Each of them recorded the four required videos. I do not think they were their best performances, but they had worked on them. I was obviously very frustrated with this teaching approach because it contradicted not only my experience but also research data indicating that students do not join a music ensemble to practice alone. They join a music ensemble because they want to belong, be in community, and make music together. The band lessons were completely void of the ensemble experience; there was no meaning or reason to practice individually. After our sons submitted their lessons, a few days before final grades were due, they learned the total number of recorded videos should have been eight, not four. To our surprise, both of our sons earned a 67 in band, which in New York State was the suggested grade for students who were not able to finish any assignments for their classes after moving to remote instruction.

Despite my frustration as a parent and as a music educator, our family made peace with the lowest grades our sons have ever received in band. I did not reach out to the band director or the principal to complain or request a better grade. We were OK with their 67. In the end, that grade was not important. What was important were matters of life and death. What the band teacher did not know was that in less than a month, two of our relatives had died of COVID-19 complications in Brazil. Their funerals and memorial services were transmitted via Zoom; their burials were streamed via FaceTime with only four of our cousins there. They died alone in hospitals far away from their hometowns, unconscious, intubated, removed from everyone they loved. What our family really needed was to heal, mourn, and be together. We needed to restore faith in our humanity and our love for each other. And we did just that.

In the fall of 2020, our senior moved on to St. Bonaventure University, a Division I athletic institution, where he joined the swimming and diving team and began his classes in-person. Our sophomore attended in-person classes two days a week at the high school and three days remotely. An awarded track and field athlete, he was discouraged by the cancellation of fall sports. As for music, he dropped out of band but remained in chorus and had a rewarding experience singing with the auditioned choir. I am grateful for the choral teacher who worked tirelessly to engage students with the subject matter when it was so tempting to let music disappear in the virtual environment. I am grateful that she understood that music ensemble is about community, even if it is a virtual one. I am even more grateful for the opportunity to focus on what really matters in these difficult times.

CHAPTER 25

UNEXPECTED "BONUS TIME"

Edmund "Ted" Hamann

I am a parent (or, more aptly, a co-parent) to a 20-year-old and 23-year-old. While the pandemic has not dramatically changed my parenting of my daughter, the older of the two, who no longer lives in our home, the pandemic has unexpectedly impacted how my partner and I parent our son. At the last minute, on March 14, 2020, I drove to St. Paul, Minnesota to pick him up from college. That date was supposed to be the first day of his spring break and, as late as March 7, he had expected to spend March 14 arriving in Madrid Spain, where he was going to meet his girlfriend who had been spending her Spring semester on a study abroad in Granada Spain. Those plans had fallen apart in the week leading to the 14th and his mother and I felt rather lucky that he hadn't arrived in Spain just as the pandemic was taking off there and international travel was shutting down.

So in mid-March I made the six-hour drive from our home in Lincoln Nebraska to St. Paul and then, after two hours of packing our minivan, turned around and drove him, all of his clothes and books, and his pet fish (the only "pet" his college allows) back home. At that point, his college had not yet decided that the remainder of the semester would be remote. I guess then it was my second parenting decision related to COVID (the first was to go get him) to tell him to pack everything, as neither his mother

Parenting in the Pandemic: The Collision of School, Work, and Life at Home, pp. 117–120

117

nor I anticipated that he would be allowed back any time soon. Apparently we were prescient.

Since mid-March (eight months ago at the time of this writing), we have reverted from being an "empty nest" to in-person parents to a college student. There has been a large overlay these eight months of a kind of ironic thankfulness for what my partner calls "bonus time" with our son at home. We get to have long conversations about the election, about his plans for the future, why he has become a vegetarian, and myriad other things that just wouldn't happen if he was two states or further away. This bonus comes even as we lament his missed opportunities and restlessness—his plans to spend summer 2020 working in Ecuador and the fall as an exchange student in China have gone out the window. More substantially, we grieve the broader havoc that the pandemic and America's fumbling response have co-generated. We are far from the most impacted Americans in relation to COVID-19—I have two high school friends who have gotten sick and better, one a long-hauler; my partner's great uncle is currently hospitalized; my son's girlfriend's roommate has tested positive—but so far no close deaths. Knock on wood.

While it may always be misleading to use the verb *guided* to describe logics for our parenting (as, in my experience, parenting is always a hybrid of intent, instinct, and improvisation with "guided" really only tightly related to the first of these three), we have tried to remember in our newest parenting role that the previous plan had been for our son to be away these months. Acquiescing to the loose *in loco parentis* logic that prevails in residential liberal arts colleges, we had been ready to trust and mostly financially support him quite far from our oversight. He wouldn't have had a curfew at college. So he doesn't have one with us, though if he is going to be away overnight or back quite late, we ask for a text. That's not to restrict him, but rather for us to have peace of mind if we wake up and see his bed still empty.

Two weeks after he came home, his classes resumed as remote instruction. Hearing and seeing him logged on his laptop meant that we were more aware of his attending to school, or not, than we would have been. But we have been reluctant to do more than ask what he is studying, what assignment he has pending, and how it feels to learn in this changed format. (He doesn't like it.) This posture has been an easy one to maintain as he seems to have been persevering with his studies, but what would we have done if the switch to remote learning had been more trepidatious for him? Frankly, I don't know. Reverted to the naggy parenting that encouraged homework completion in high school?

This summer he did not have classes and he spent much of his time continuing a job at Walmart as a personal shopper that he had begun shortly after he came home. Apart from worrying about his mask wearing and other precautions (and he has seemed pretty diligent about being careful), our parenting role related to that work has been pretty limited. From time to time, we lent him a car to get there, but often he biked. The original plan at the end of the summer was to leave Walmart and return to college, a proposition that his school had consistently labeled as contingent on the advice of Minnesota's Department of Health. As his college made plans to rent an entire hotel and use it as a student athletes' dorm, we continued to check in with him and approved of his decision to not join his sophomore roommate in looking for off-campus housing, as it sounded like his housing plan was settled. Late in the summer, however, his college decided to abandon the plan for renting a hotel, cancelled all intercollegiate athletics for the semester, and announced that only first-year students, international students, and those without secure home settings would be welcome on campus. All classes would again be remote.

This was concurrently understandable and disappointing news, but for us it meant 'bonus time' has continued. Even though he was staying in Nebraska for another semester, he decided to leave the Walmart job in late August to become instead a waiter at a local restaurant-bar. We worried about whether this would increase his exposure (and eventually our exposure) to COVID-19, but he explained that he would be interacting with a much smaller number of people, that he would be working fewer hours but earning just as much (also allowing time for his resumed studies), and that most diners were choosing to eat on the restaurant's outdoor patio because they too felt safer outdoors rather than in. Our parenting again seemed to mainly be talking through his reasoning for various actions and checking how he was keeping safe.

This fall his classes have been taught remotely and mostly he hasn't liked that. His professors are struggling with the changed format (teaching at a liberal arts college usually means intense and enjoyable in-person instruction), and we struggle with how encouraging to be. With the Spring 2021 semester shaping up to again be taught remotely, he has decided to take a leave of absence from college and has enrolled in an in-person Wilderness EMT class taught in Wyoming by the National Outdoor Leadership School and, after that is completed, he wants to look for an internship in a solar energy-related company. We'll see how that works out, but we like the idea that he is driving the planning and attempting to make lemonade from lemons. He still intends to finish college on time (in May 2022), but he likely will need to drop his second declared major—Chinese—because the blockage of his chances to study abroad there mean he's not getting an immersion experience to substantially advance his language skills and to check off several of the Chinese culture and history requirements that are also part of the major. I guess parenting has partially transformed into delighting about his emerging attentiveness, knowing we could step in, but thinking it's better if we don't.

About a month ago, there was a pandemic-related hiccup. His long-time girlfriend, who has also been part of our substantially reduced social bubble, reported that her roommate, a paraprofessional in the local school system had tested positive for COVID and was mildly symptomatic. So we then had our son and his girlfriend quarantine together in our basement as they were tested multiple times for COVID and waited out the timeline from their known exposure. Our basement was an easier space to distance from the roommate than her apartment would have been, but directly providing cohabitation is not a line of parent decision-making that we would have been pursuing absent the pandemic.

Even more recently, as COVID has been spiking locally and nationally and colder weather is driving more restaurant traffic indoors, we strongly encouraged him to drop the waitering job pointing out that his heightened risk-taking would become our de facto heightened risk taking too. He agreed and we helped him set up a temporary job delivering bread for a neighbor's bakery (we knew that that neighbor's regular driver had just had to start quarantining). I guess then another part of "bonus time" parenting isn't just advising and consulting but troubleshooting too. Maybe "guided" is an apt word for this instance.

I realize that for others, the pandemic has driven much bigger and much more harrowing changes in parenting than we have had to negotiate. We often feel lucky (and guilty) that this pandemic has arrived after our children were small and needed much more protection. Still, COVID-19 has changed parenting of college students too, and a holistic effort to chronicle the pandemic's impact on parenting would be incomplete without this portion of the story too.

SECTION III

"WE ARE HERE FOR THE STORM":
SEEKING BALANCE IN THE MIDST OF CRISIS

... There's an umbrella
by the door, not for yesterday but for the weather that's here ...
... We are here for the storm
That's storming because what's taken matters.

—Claudia Rankine, Weather

There is hope in definition. There is hope in origin. *Quarantine* comes from
the Latin meaning forty days. How long has it been and how long will
it be and is it the same kind of forty as from the ark and the flood, the
devil in the desert and the forty-hour workweek? How will we will
our lives into something more?

—Tommy Orange, Aftermaths[1]

The pandemic has brought disruption and upheaval to our lives in many ways. As academics and parents, we are accustomed to the juggle of work and home. School closures, remote learning, and working from home have upended the carefully constructed routines that have taken years to establish. In the midst of tragedy, we are also plagued by the mundane, everyday

---

details of life in the pandemic. As we navigate the flood of demands on our time, our search for balance has led us to create new parenting routines, identify hidden crevices of time in our days for work, and shift our priorities. To draw on Claudia Rankine's use of weather imagery to describe the pandemic, many of us have reached for and opened umbrellas we didn't know we had, recreating our work and lives to respond to the storm. As we do so, we mourn the loss of what has been taken from us at the same time that we find new meaning in the daily rhythms, the joy of a family meal or the early morning walk, trying to "will our lives into something more," as Tommy Orange describes this time in quarantine.

The essays in this section show the many ways we are weathering this storm. Pandemic parenting has required us to reconfigure the careful puzzle pieces of our daily lives. Whether we are co-parents, stepparents, or single parents, we find ourselves juggling the increased responsibilities that arrive with the pandemic even as our work obligations seem to continue at a relentless pace. As professors, we have more flexibility than most to construct our daily routines, deciding when, where and how to work most of the time. We are well-practiced in prioritization, balancing teaching, and research, carving out our most productive writing time, and crafting our own work schedules around the rhythms of our families. Even so, the pandemic knocked us off our feet, upending the routines, piling on new responsibilities, and leaving us with little, if any, uninterrupted time for work. The essays in this section speak to that disruption, examining the ways in which we have grappled with the changing routines and demands of the pandemic.

These essays also reveal the duality of this time, as we reflect on the meaning of this time. The essays illustrate powerful insights about how this impossible balance has created a set of paradoxes for us all, unresolvable in the dilemmas we face. Some reflect on the ways we are learning about ourselves and our children during this time. Others find calm in the eye of the storm, grateful for the rare quiet moment to reflect on our priorities. We carry both grief and gratitude as we remake our lives in the midst of crisis. As we seek balance and try to make sense of the weather, as Rankine puts it, we find ways to frame this disruption as a form of renewal and recentering.

ENDNOTE

1. Both poems come from a timely volume of poetry about the pandemic, *Together in a Sudden Strangeness: America's Poets Respond to the Pandemic* (Quinn, 2021), which played a role in inspiring this book.

CHAPTER 26

PARADOXES IN PANDEMIC PARENTING

Martin Scanlan

In the spring of 2020, just as COVID-19 was unsettling the rhythms of life, I discovered comedian Tom Papa on the radio show Live from Here. Each week Papa would deliver a monologue, "Out in America," recounting travel to cities across the U.S. where he sought out everyday people. In a deadpan delivery he would describe his encounters, employing a trademark line to punctuate particularly wacky moments: "Have you ever ... I have." For instance, in San Diego, looking out over the ocean and listening to a bartender extol his glorious carefree surfing world, Papa mused: "Have you ever found yourself drinking a mystery drink out of a blowfish and start thinking that maybe you've been living your life all wrong? I have."

In the summer of 2020 Live From Here was canceled—a COVID casualty—abruptly ending my enjoyment of "Out in America." And while I missed the weekly armchair traveling of Papa's comic tales, I also had begun realizing that daily life in the pandemic was punctuated with scenes that could be straight out of his routine. I started musing variations on his question, "Have you ever...?" Sometimes mine were light: "Have you ever found yourself noticing that an unintended benefit of your children wearing a facemask is that they pay much closer attention to their oral

Parenting in the Pandemic: The Collision of School, Work, and Life at Home, pp. 123–126
Copyright © 2021 by Information Age Publishing

hygiene? I have." Other times they were heavier: "Have you ever found yourself lying awake in the middle of the night fretting over how each of your children are missing their commencements from elementary, middle, and high school? I have."

I think what attracted me to Papa's schtick was that in a simple, wry manner, it playfully presented some of life's paradoxes. Paradox—combining the Greek prefix *para-* ("beyond or" "outside of ") with the verb *dokein* ("to think")—connotes thinking in a manner that counters expectations, often juxtaposing contrasting experiences. And paradoxes, in my view, are the bread and butter of parenting in the pandemic.

Spending days, weeks, months on end together in our abode, our three children, wife, and our aging dog—I find small paradoxes abound. Forced together in tight quarters all day leaves my son feeling trapped, but then he comes downstairs and joins his brother and me to play pool, and we're suddenly feeling a little less constricted. Limited from seeing friends makes my daughter lonelier, but then she whiles away hours creating art and feels some peace. Losing the communal gathering of our weekly scramble to get to Sunday mass, we find ourselves haphazardly, casually creating a new familial ritual, sitting together in the living room with a candle, a reading, a song. At once trapped but free, bored but creative, isolated yet bonded ... I find parenting in the pandemic punctuated by simple, day-in, day-out paradoxes. Most are minor, inconsequential, fleeting.

But on occasion, a paradox has crept up that is more substantive: Have you ever found yourself at the end of another Groundhog Day of pandemic living, shaking off the day's virtual world of school and work, trying to maintain some semblance of civility around the dinner table with everyone's nerves more than a little frayed, and suddenly starting to think that what the family really needs right now to get through this rough time is to raise a new puppy? I have.

I don't know who gets credit—or blame—for suggesting the idea. In hindsight, I think it had been lingering for years in the background, like the vat of kraut on the kitchen counter, slowly fermenting, biding its time. Then, one day, someone took off the lid and gave it a taste: is it ready? Fiona, our aging Australian Shepherd, was increasingly lethargic, a shadow of her former self. Wouldn't it make sense to get a puppy now, so the old pooch could nurture the young pup? Perhaps this would even help rekindle some of Fiona's spunk! And what better time than now, when we're all stuck at home and have time to devote to training? The conversation around the dinner table grew increasingly animated, and in short order the idea had taken on a momentum of inevitability.

And so it began: the journey of bringing in a new creature to the home. For weeks the children bantered about names—lobbying each other to try to build voting blocks. We hunted for accoutrements, finding a used crate on a listserve, a small traveling bag from a neighbor, new toys, and chow at the pet store. A sense of expectation swept into our pandemic-weary household. The children—two teens and a tween—were young again, giddily gazing at the phone when a picture of their newborn pup arrived, eagerly counting down the weeks till she could come home.

Have you ever watched your children wait for months with mounting excitement over the arrival of a new pet, earnestly assuring you that they understand the responsibility this will entail and pledging full commitment to walking and feeding and caring for this new member of the household, and then within a few hours of the pet's homecoming realize that they were actually totally lying to you? I have.

Pepper arrived home the second week of July. It didn't take long for the family to realize that a puppy in theory is a cute cuddle, but a puppy in practice is a constant chore. The interrupted sleep, the inevitable accidents, the constant chewing … all to be expected, of course. But having always adopted rescue dogs who were older, I'd never really thought about how much work a youngster would be. And while I like to complain that the brunt of the dirty work falls on me, the truth of the matter is that as Pepper has become a part of the family over the last few months, she has transformed my children. As they have in so many other ways—navigating online schooling, maintaining friendships remotely, fastidiously protecting their health—the children keep learning to adapt to new expectations and assume new responsibilities.

Pandemic or not, parenting seems to inevitably entail facing paradox. In this time of vulnerability and unrest, of uncertainty and ambiguity, of discombobulation, I wanted to simplify. I wanted to minimize the moving parts—not add more. But bringing this new little life into the home has not just complicated our family. It has nourished us as well. Pepper's daily walks force us to get out. Wrestling with her chew toys provides a welcome respite from the computer screens. Even in the continued cleaning of accidents we can—when we're at our best—ruefully grin at each other and laugh at ourselves. With her full body wag and irrepressible yip, she models for us all an unconditional affection that we too yearn to express.

Like everyone, I am looking forward to the days when this pandemic is behind us. And with preliminary vaccines rolling out across the globe, dawn glimmers on the horizon. There is so much to forget, and so much to hope for. But as I write these words, I find Pepper sleeping at my feet, calm and quiet, and I'm reminded that grace sometimes comes in facing—even embracing—the paradoxes of life and living (see Figure 26.1).

Figure 26.1

Pepper by Clara Scanlan (Age 12)

CHAPTER 27

CHAOS AND CONNECTION

Lisa M. Dorner

These aren't normal times for parents, are they? **"Mom, I'm afraid I have COVID!"** Trying to hold back tears, these are the first words spoken by my 13-year-old daughter, Amalia, on the morning of November 14, 2020. She continues: "My throat hurts, my nose is stuffy, I have a headache." I rub my eyes. *Yes, all of these could be symptoms for COVID-19.* My brain is working slowly and quickly at the same time. My partner, Chip, isn't home. My older son, Locke, is still sleeping. It's a little before 8 a.m. I'm co-leading a virtual professional development for teachers across Missouri at 10 A.M. I try to think: *What to do, what am I supposed to do?* The thoughts keep coming: There's the Urgent Care nearby, where Locke got his COVID test last spring—thankfully negative. I try again: *But what would I **normally** do? Ah, right: take her temperature, maybe call the pediatrician. And how about: try to stay calm.* "Amalia, let's take your temp. OK, 99.2, not even considered a fever." *That's a good sign, right?* Next, I call the doctor, but I'm on hold for 45 minutes. By the time they pick up at 8:45 A.M., I'm at the Urgent Care with Amalia—where they've already run out of COVID tests for the day. Chatting with the nurse, we decide that's just as well; for the most accurate results on a rapid test, it's better if she has symptoms for 48 hours, so we decide I'll call back on Monday. We get home in time for me to lead my

Parenting in the Pandemic: The Collision of School, Work, and Life at Home, pp. 127–130

portion of the professional development via Zoom. I do my part but turn off my video periodically to check on Amalia.

I think about pre-COVID times later that afternoon, after my Zoom meetings are finished and we all don our masks. Just months ago, we simply would've made a cup of tea, taken an extra vitamin C, and went about our day. I also would not have been home, as I would have had to drive at least 30 minutes to meet with teachers in person. But these days, a sore throat sends my brain into a frenzy, and I quarantine my daughter to her room at the slightest sign of illness. Also, these days, I can be at work after a minute commute to my new bedroom-office, connecting with teachers across the state with a simple click on the internet.

And so goes pandemic parenting: swinging back and forth between chaos and connection.

I think back to the very beginning of our pandemic parenting experience: Wednesday, March 11, 2020. Spring break is soon, and we're headed to visit a few colleges for Locke, who's a junior. But one e-mail after another comes to my inbox. It feels like a slow wind that picks up into a tornado. My university, Mizzou, announces that it's cancelling all classes for two days, so professors like me can transition to 100% online learning the following Monday. *What?!* (For a laugh about this, see here: https://youtu.be/CCe5PaeAeew.) Grinnell College and other universities suspend all events, including admission tours. Doctors advise stay-at-home orders. And, finally, my kids' schools decide they'll be virtual for the two weeks after spring break, which starts the following Monday.

At this point, we begin our stay-at-home life. We're privileged without a doubt. We have jobs, solid access to medical care, (mostly) reliable internet, and a house large enough for quarantining. Chip continues working from home developing websites for small businesses and nonprofits, some that continue to hire him using stimulus funding. I have prior experience teaching online. Locke and Amalia are independent learners, which I get to watch unfold on a daily basis, as my daughter develops her own daily writing-exercise-study-baking schedule, and my son figures out how to go on virtual college-admission tours, enroll in Coursera classes for fun, and take his AP tests fully online. We join an international study about family life and learning in a pandemic, which turns into weekly, mother-daughter journal writing. There is no track season, but Chip and Locke start running together regularly. Amalia invites me to a sleep-over, where we do each other's hair and play games late into the night. We hit a family record in the number of Missouri state parks we visit. I re-realize why I love my family, and I feel so lucky to connect with them in new ways during this time; they're a funny bunch.

Of course, it was chaotic, too. *Don't believe what you see on any parent's Facebook page!* There was the Calculus AP test that had to be retaken due to a technological glitch; tears and frustration over the lack of proficient instruction and clear communication from our schools; cancellations of trips to visit my own parents, including my dad who's surviving cancer and *cannot* get COVID-19; an actual lack of flour and hand sanitizer in our stores; stressful decision-making overload as we responded to countless surveys about whether or not our kids would go to school in person; negotiations on how to get together safely with family and friends, … and no quiet time to myself. *Remember having a toddler, the beauty of seeing them grow right before your eyes, but never getting to be in the bathroom without an interruption? It's like that again, but with teenagers.*

There's also the worry for our community's ever and growing racial and economic disparities. As an education researcher, I know what's happening in my house is just one story. Both my kids attend racially diverse public magnet schools, which have experienced leadership, dedicated staff, and well-funded Parent-Teacher Organizations —but there's quite a far way to go for equity in St. Louis.[1] Our district spent most of the spring getting food to families, much less devices for virtual learning. In the fall, we joined **50 other volunteers** to make sure all families at a nearby elementary school received their devices, supplies, and online training to start school. The disparities in education always existed, but the pandemic accentuated the very real daily chaos—and lack of connections—experienced by too many in our society.

Flash back to November 2020, two days after Amalia got sick. On Monday, she still has cold symptoms, so we get her tested, even though she's had no contact with any COVID cases. Turns out she's positive; *asymptomatic spread is real, eh*. I question every decision we made as parents. We do our own contact tracing. I re-weigh and re-weigh the risks and benefits of having let her continue with gymnastics, the only thing she was doing outside of the house inside another building—but, without a mask. I see firsthand the failure of our policies and practices, especially the continued lack of testing, nonexistent contact tracing, no state mask mandate, and disregard for our area's pandemic task force warnings and recommendations. I wonder how we got here, as a family, as a society.

But, in spite of this most serious chaos and disruption, we manage to stop the infection with Amalia; no one else got sick. And I work to remember the new connections and growth of these times: the creative online Zooming; the outdoor bike-riding and camping; watching Locke and Amalia as they manage their new circumstances—and recognizing that they know more about how to get through life than we may often credit them. **And so we go on, learning as parents through chaos and connection.**

Figure 27.1

Social Distancing by Amalia Meyer

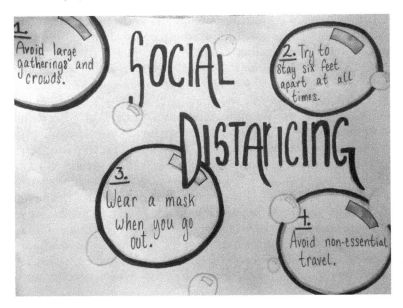

ENDNOTE

1. For comparable situations, check out Nice White Parents, www.nytimes.com/2020/07/30/podcasts/nice-white-parents-serial.html and The Promise, wpln.org/programs/the-promise.)

CHAPTER 28

SINGLE-PARENTING AS AN ACADEMIC DURING A GLOBAL HEALTH PANDEMIC

Lessons Learned About Managing Distraction, Mom Guilt, and Self-Compassion

Sera J. Hernandez

As school was being rewritten due to a global pandemic, I braced myself for the likely upheaval that the pandemic would have on my home and work life. The stress of juggling multiple professional and personal roles as a single-mother academic were present before the pandemic, but were exacerbated with the realities of COVID-19. In addition to the health pandemic, the anti-Black racism pandemic, albeit ongoing, exploded in front of our eyes after the murder of George Floyd, Ahmaud Arbery, Breonna Taylor, and others. While managing the expectations of academia with my children's zoom schedules and other daily routines has been maddening at times, I will focus on the opportunities the pandemic has offered us as a family, and particularly me as an academic mother.

Parenting in the Pandemic: The Collision of School, Work, and Life at Home, pp. 131–135
Copyright © 2021 by Information Age Publishing

COVID-19 brought a major change to my work reality: my kids were now my coworkers. But unlike my experiences with coworkers on campus, I am unable to close my office door or truly reap the benefits of noise-cancelling headphones. My daughter is in fifth grade and her new classroom is the bedroom that she and her brother share. She sits at a tiny desk at the foot of their bunk bed. The first few weeks of the pandemic she would pack a lunch (e.g., heat up lentils and rice and put it in a thermos, include some snacks and shove them in her lunch bag) before starting her 9:00 A.M. zoom call. Sometimes I walk into her room to see her reading a book under the desk while "in class." My son is in second grade and his new classroom is our living room. He takes his zoom calls from our coffee table. He has a hard time sitting for more than five minutes, and when I walk through the living room to get from my "office" (kitchen) to the bathroom, I see him rolling around on the couch. And, perhaps because there is now a stove/oven in my office, I turned into Betty Crocker during the onset of the pandemic, baking Amish Friendship Bread every 10 days (for months) and serving up 5-course meals to my children a few times a week. It is clear this was one way of coping with the stay-at-home orders.

In addition to the baking, there were two main realizations I made early on in the pandemic that helped me cope. First, I was able to draw on my 20+ years of experience and learning in education, with roles that include teacher, counselor, professional developer, teacher educator, and university professor. As a scholar trained in sociocultural frameworks of education, I have a deep understanding that learning happens everywhere (not just in schools) and learning happens with multiple individuals (not just teachers). This is not to say that schools and teachers are not valuable, but I was able to not buy into the fear that my children were going to fall behind or miss some state-sanctioned benchmark because of distance learning. I saw the pandemic as an opportunity for me to lean into my parenting in a way that honored my children's unique spirits and talents, and continue to learn how to live with and love them in a more responsive way. However, I also realized that we have created a huge injustice in letting many parents, guardians, and communities believe that the learning that matters most is that which happens in schools. This is especially the case for historically minoritized populations, such as immigrant and BIPOC communities.

Second, I realized that my high tolerance for ambiguity—the ability to adapt to unknown circumstances, greatly supported my ability to cope with our new normal. My tolerance for ambiguity has been developed through multiple life experiences, including being the oldest of eight children in my family and living for brief periods in different countries as an adult. But I think it was the personal grief that I experienced during my first years as an academic that has particularly required that I flex this muscle. My sister was diagnosed with leukemia while I was in my PhD program and she passed away while I was on the academic job market. A couple of years after starting my tenure track position, I went through a lengthy and traumatic divorce. Trusting the (grief and healing) process of difficult life events comes from leaning into the uncomfortable nature of the process.

While the pandemic has not made life easier, it has provided me with some opportunities for growth and healing. Having the practice of sitting still with discomfort and the unknown provided me with the skills and belief that my children and I would be just fine during the pandemic (coupled with my class privilege and steady income). When the occasional fearful thought would enter my mind (e.g., What if my children are with their father when the state goes on lockdown? When will I see them again?), I could draw on my past experiences of surviving and thriving post-divorce. I could embrace the stance that fear was not going to take over my experiences as a single-mother during a pandemic. I did not need to exacerbate reality with the potentiality of events (which is one of the reasons I never stocked up on TP). And undoubtedly, the benefits of seeking joy and centering gratitude every day (shout out to my therapist!) have supported me tremendously. I make it a daily practice to write down three things I am grateful for and I share it with my children during our breakfast. They witness me sharing what I value about them (e.g., I am grateful for my son's help with the dishes yesterday. I appreciate the dance party I had with my daughter last night.) and I invite them to write in their gratitude journals when the spirit moves them. I am also able to experience the joy of watching my kids' classroom learning in action, something I was not able to do before the pandemic. With the guidance of their thoughtful teachers, my children dance, sing, problem solve, read out loud, write stories, and contribute to class discussions daily. And because they attend a bilingual school, they do this in both English and Spanish. It is truly beautiful to witness.

Drawing on these ways of knowing (and not-knowing), centering gratitude, and leaning into the joy of parenting during a pandemic have been helpful, but I still face regular challenges with this new normal. The most significant challenges have been (1) the psychological management of interruptions/distraction and (2) regular waves of mom guilt. Distraction is something I battle regularly as an academic mother. Raising and caring for young children at any point in time has its challenges, but as the head of my household who is planning meals, shopping, paying bills, and making appointments, I am often overwhelmed with juggling multiple tasks and responsibilities. Research has documented the disproportionate impact on the productivity of female and non-binary parents who often carry the load of the caregiving responsibilities, even in two-parent households. My personal experience has been that pre- and post-divorce, I am shouldering most of the behind the scenes parenting labor. I struggle daily with what is required of me as a mom and academic (and I go up for tenure soon) since the deep focus needed to produce scholarship is on the chopping block when kids are always available to pop into the office with a "Mom, I need help" and "Can I get on the iPad?" When my kids ask for more tech time while I am writing an academic paper, prepping for my online courses, or grading assignments for students with no other caretaker in the house, I have to navigate the moment-to-moment decisions on what is best for our family. These interruptions and distractions are closely linked to the suffocating amounts of mom guilt I also manage when preparing a meal that is not the healthiest or when I give in to more technology time for the kids on the days my work schedule is unforgiving.

Today, I am better able to understand that as we navigate these complex and trying times, we are all asking for compassion. This shared human experience can help us reimagine not just schooling, but our ways of parenting, loving, and living. With or without a pandemic, single-parenting as an academic will always present challenges, and I am grateful for the resources I have to support my family amidst these challenges. And thanks to these uncertain times, I have the opportunity to hone my emerging skill of self-compassion which has helped me manage the distraction of homeschooling and offer the grace and forgiveness we all need every day, especially in 2020.

Figure 28.1

Life in Quarantine by Savannah Christine Moore

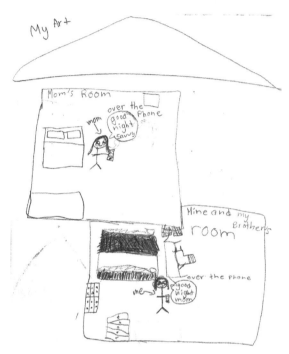

Ever since Covid-19, mom has turned the kicthen
Into her office and she does all of
her Zooms in there. I, on the other hand
do my zooms in my room on a desk. And my
Brother does his zooms in the living
room on the coffee table. This one
time my mom thoght she had Covid-19
So we called each other any time we
had some thing to say. Her test results
came back negative and She kissed me
Soi much that I had lipstick all over
my face.

CHAPTER 29

PARTICLES AND DUELING FRENCH HORNS

Sharon Dotger

Pandemic parenting means agreeing to write this essay and then being interrupted so often that…

… oh, wait. What was I doing again?

It also means …

… feeling trapped, sometimes, in this house. I want this space that I co-create with my spouse and my children to be a home that thrives with love and support. The pandemic has challenged me to live up to that goal. I never thought of myself as anti-social, but I want time alone and it has been so hard to come by. All the things I usually do to keep myself in order are no longer available. I tried allowing myself a pedicure three months ago and was so nervous the entire time that I would either get COVID or spread it that I could not relax. I have been an avid gym goer for seven years—it has really helped me focus and decompress—but I just cannot bring myself to walk in. I tried going to a workout once after the restrictions were lifted and I was so nervous that I kept having to talk myself in to staying in the room and finishing. I am trying to do the workouts at home, but I constantly get interrupted. Olympic lifting is not the same when you are worried about dropping the barbell on your kid.

… feeling constantly guilty that I am never in the right place doing the right thing at the right time. Previously, when the guilt of being a working mom was strong, I thought I would revel in having months with my chil-

Parenting in the Pandemic: The Collision of School, Work, and Life at Home, pp. 137–139
Copyright © 2021 by Information Age Publishing

dren. I have been home with the two of them now for eight months. When it's good, it is fun, and I am thankful for my time with them. But when I am frustrated with the things you get frustrated with as a parent—repeating yourself, asking questions that are never answered, the constant interruptions, there is nowhere to go—literally—to get away from them and reset. I realize now, more than before, that when I was able to go to campus and they were in school, our separate locations made it feel okay that we were not together. We were where we were supposed to be. However, now, I feel like I'm living that scene in *This is 40* where Paul Rudd is playing a game while sitting on the toilet—all the time I get to myself, including the minutes I am spending on these sentences, feels like it is time I am stealing away in shame. I feel shame if I am working. I feel shame if I am not.

… feeling frustrated that I should bend myself into shapes more complex than pretzels to support my kids' teachers. But then, I must listen to the kids watch a brainpop video for the umpteenth time in a week or witness them complete another worksheet in another packet and I just want to cry. This kind of instruction is so far afield of what I usually advocate for professionally. It seems on the one hand that I should forgive this instructional poverty amid an emergency and yet I know it just a digital extension of what was happening before it started. It's just now saying something seems worse because of the pandemic. Or I forget to check each of their band schedules and schedule a zoom presentation while they both have French horn lessons. One plays Smash Mouth, the other the Star Wars theme, and I am trying to talk to colleagues around the country about teacher professional development.

… feeling confused. I am so uncertain about managing risk. As I write this, cases are on an exponential rise again. I have pulled my kids into fully online instruction; we are not participating in any sporting events. People I trust are making other choices – and I do not want my choices to seem like a referendum on their own – but I question if I am being appropriately or overly cautious. I wonder about the limits I have placed on how my kids use their devices, since the device is currently their line to connect with others. If I feel like I need some space from the kids without guilt, I bet they feel the same about me.

… feeling really pissed off. My children are crying about the politics of our country right now. They fear for their civil rights, they fear for the rights of their friends. They are afraid of the people in the flak jackets with the guns in front of polling places, the threat of a governor kidnapped, and a substantial proportion of the population denying truth. They tell me they feel safe in our home, but they do not feel safe in the world.

And yet, we talk about …

… how to care about others, to give and expect consent, to rise above self-interest and work for the good of the whole.

... how important community is and the need to support others, to establish means to help when things are hard.

... truth. Yes, the virus is real. Yes, the virus is airborne. Yes, your mother is a science educator and will do her damnedest to help you build a particle model of matter because particle models are really useful for understanding why masks work and why air flow can make a difference in lowering risk of transmission (take a breath, Sharon – get your particles). No, race has no basis in biology, but yes, it is very real. Yes, there are differences in how citizens get access to vote. Yes, your parents will vote and when you are old enough, you will, too.

And we ...

... sew masks to give to the hospital and to friends
... bake for ourselves and our neighbors
... videocall loved ones
... plan road trips to take when it is safe to do again
... protest injustice and brutality
... listen to music
... quilt
... read
... hope
... hug.

Figure 29.1

Quarantine by Annie Dotger (age 14)

CHAPTER 30

STRUGGLING BEAUTIFULLY

Raising Two Black Girls in the Midst of Global Health and Racial Pandemics

Terrance L. Green

Being a father is something that I hold dearly to my heart. For me, fatherhood carries weighty responsibilities, opportunities, and great promise. With my wife (life partner), raising two Black girls, ages 1 and 4-years-old, has been the most beautiful and marvelous yet difficult and arduous experience that we have ever embarked upon. However, during 2020, the good, bad, and everything in-between as a parent and academic was tested.

As a Black father in America, I was born into a pandemic of racial and anti-Black oppression that gained mainstream attention in 2020 with the countless unarmed killings of Black people by law enforcement and white vigilantes. At the same time, the pandemic of COVID-19 spread throughout the world taking the lives of millions of people, shutting down countries, and shifting the ways that people work, and frankly do life. This has caused me to constantly feel a range of emotions such as uncertainty, rage, disappointment, anger, and stress. Yet, I am finding solace through three practices that I am learning to embrace which I describe as *struggling*

Parenting in the Pandemic: The Collision of School, Work, and Life at Home, pp. 141–143
Copyright © 2021 by Information Age Publishing
All rights of reproduction in any form reserved.

beautifully as a parent and academic. To me, struggling beautifully is a gift that accounts for the difficulties, tears, heartaches, and losses as well as the triumphs, joys, and blessings that the year 2020 brought.

Finding Beauty in Death

On September 13, 2020, I watched my grandmother take her last three breaths. Three. Two. One. And like that her life on this side of eternity expired—and according to my faith system—her life on the other side of eternity began. This was an extremely tough loss for my family and myself because my grandmother was the matriarch of our family. She was part of the first generation that was born in Detroit in 1934 after her parents had migrated from the South in pursuit of a better life. Right after her passing, I put my face in the palms of my hands and began to cry and give thanks for her life. It was a moment of struggle yet great beauty that continues to have a profound impact on me. This experience is causing me to reflect on and ask deep questions about how much time I have left, my parenting, my life's work, and a host of other things. Death has a way of bringing things that were out of focus back into clarity, and strangely enough, is doing so for me.

My Presence Is My Best Present

With all of the changes that 2020 brought, our children could no longer go to daycare and are still at home with us while my wife and I are working (or attempting to work). For the first six years of my professional life, working to earn tenure made me a workaholic. Seemingly, every moment of spare time that I had was devoted to finishing a manuscript, thinking about a manuscript, collecting data for a manuscript, or putting together a presentation based on a manuscript. But even after earning tenure, I am coming to realize that old habits die slowly. I still find myself in front of my laptop more than I would like to. As a result, my four-year-old daughter often says things like, "daddy, please get off of your computer" or "daddy, are you on your computer again?" This creates feelings of guilt, frustration, and at times sentiments of misprioritization that are constantly there.

And of course, to them our work encroached upon all of the time that my daughters thought would be spent with them. However, throughout this year, with the help, suggestions, and loving support from some friends and family, I have come to realize (even though I still don't practice it to the degree to which I realize it) that my presence is the best present that I could give to my daughters. While this is still a struggle at times for me, setting work aside for some time to be fully present with my daughters has been marvelous. I have come to witness the joys of my 4-year-old daughter developing a deep love for track and field, specifically jumping over baby hurdles to imitate her daddy. I have also come to see the amazing beauty on my 1-year-old daughter's face when I make funny noises with my lips that she tries to mimic while laughing profusely. I have also come to see the joys on my wife's face as she laughs uncontrollably when I do some of my unique dances. Despite the emotional struggles of guilt and frustration, I have found breakthroughs of joy in the midst of it all. Sometimes it is harder to find, but it is there.

Pictures Are Artifacts of Life and Catalogs of History

Everything that happened in 2020 caused me to think about the ways that I parent. Given that time is so finite and that our memories are so precious it's imperative to capture snapshots of the time that we are afforded with our family, but specifically with our children, while we can. Therefore, one of the practices that I learned from a colleague is to take as many pictures and videos as possible of my family and children right now. This practice, which is something that I *try* to do daily (although I still don't), is to take at least one picture or video of my children and then watch/look at them every few weeks as a family. I have come to realize that pictures are precious artifacts of our lives and catalogs of our histories that can bring joy, laughter, and smiles to myself, my wife, and children. As we look through the pictures and watch the videos we realize that there are a myriad of beautiful moments in the midst of all of the struggling and loss that we experienced in 2020 such as joy-filled times of laughter, growth, and family love.

In sum, not only did these two pandemics alter the course of the world but they also altered my parenting and work as an academic. The coexistence of struggle and beauty create a lot of tensions, contradictions, and paradoxes for me as a parent and academic. However, the moments that reside in my mind, my spirit, and in my overall life are actually gifts that emerged in the midst of struggling beautifully in 2020.

CHAPTER 31

LOCKDOWN

Alexandra Freidus

Before I was a mom or a professor, I was a teacher. I vividly remember going into my first classroom in August 2005, determined to make it feel like home. On March 16, 2020, my New York City apartment became my classroom. My 8-year-old needed to continue third grade remotely, and his little brother was determined to do school alongside him.

That first week, my kids sat across from each other at the kitchen table. Each morning, we made a schedule for the big kid's tasks: math practice (his favorite), reading (which he didn't consider schoolwork), writing (a real struggle). His teacher sent home a folder the Friday before the lockdown began, fearing that it was imminent. Sunday evening, when the mayor announced the school closings, she e-mailed us a plan for working through the packets. As his big brother checked items off his lists, the preschooler busily drew pictures and completed dot-to-dots.

One evening that week, our family sat down together and made a list of things we wanted to do during lockdown when we weren't "doing school." The goals were reasonable: practice the recorder; take hikes; preschool Zoom yoga; make a new cookie recipe; write letters to family. We figured we would get through the list before school reopened in a month or so. I planned our days precisely, stayed up past midnight working, and silently congratulated myself for applying what I'd learned about structures and

Parenting in the Pandemic: The Collision of School, Work, and Life at Home, pp. 145–149
Copyright © 2021 by Information Age Publishing

routines from years of classroom teaching. My partner, an essential worker who continued to commute several times a week, deferred to my "expert knowledge."

When "Zoom school" began two weeks later, I set the 8-year-old up on my laptop. He was thrilled—he'd never been allowed to touch my computer before. I eavesdropped as he told his classmates that the best thing about the week was having his mom be his teacher. I beamed.

I'm still not exactly sure when things changed.

Was it in early April when my partner got really ill, couldn't take a full breath, and lost his sense of smell? Was it 10 days later, when he was finally upright but I was suddenly unable to stand for more than 10 minutes as a time? Our routines certainly suffered during that time.

Was it when our next-door neighbors—an elderly family of three—passed away? We were barely leaving the house, so the kids had no opportunity to notice. But the grown-ups locked ourselves up in the bedroom, whispering, while they got hours of unprecedented TV time. They definitely noticed that. And they heard the sirens round the clock for weeks on end.

Was it when Zoom shifted from an occasional novelty to the new normal? All I know for sure is that within a month, the preschooler hid when I said it was time to do yoga. And the big kid started shouting at us angrily after every remote morning meeting. After a week or so, he told me that he didn't want to do Zoom anymore. It made him too sad that he couldn't play with friends. We tried hiding the square that showed his face, then turning off his own video, then listening in without watching the meeting. No dice.

Soon, our entire household was swinging on a wild pendulum. There would be periods each day—hours, sometimes—of total calm, in large part because the third-grader was lost in a book. He read the entire Percy Jackson series, once, then again. I marveled at his focus, feeling incredibly lucky. And then it would be time for us to "do some school." Computers were violently slammed shut, books hurled across the room, packets that I had spent hours printing torn in half.

In many ways, my kid had a best-case scenario for distanced learning: a highly-skilled, extremely dedicated third-grade teacher who labored late every night after her own two kids had gone to bed to create engaging online curricula; two parents with relatively flexible job responsibilities who could offer support at home; a professional educator mom who knew how to plan a school day and break down instructional tasks. It didn't seem to matter.

One day at lunch in late April, the big kid looked up at me and my partner and suddenly started sobbing. When we asked what was wrong, he choked out that he didn't want us to die.

Soon after, we decided to pretty much stop "doing school." I sadly told his teacher that from then on, he would join only one class meeting each week. Every Wednesday at 10 A.M., we set a recurring seven-minute timer together. When it rang, his dad or I would come by, check that he was minimally engaged on Zoom, and silently hand him two Sour Patch Kids. He dutifully logged onto the math platform each day, completing the third, then the fourth, then the fifth-grade lessons. And that was it.

I firmly told myself what I would have said to anybody else in our situation. This was only temporary. His academics were fine, beyond fine. Our family's well-being mattered most. Besides, there is so much more to learning than school can ever offer. Yet I worried aloud, almost constantly, to my partner about our kid's lagging writing, which he protested practicing more virulently than ever before—and his slipping social skills, as he went a week at a time without talking to anybody his age. My professional judgement could not relieve my anxiety in a world with no good options.

When I managed to put my own fears aside, I worried much more about other families. Families with parents who might not feel confident making judgement calls about what parts of school are necessary and what are not. Families with teachers that didn't trust parents to know what is in their own kids' best interests. Families of kids with learning disabilities who were missing key supports. Families without the capacity to keep an adult nearby as kids struggled with technology. Families who got much sicker than we had. Families without access to technology or secure food or housing. My own family was so privileged; our choices felt terrible, but we had choices. In a society where we have failed to collectively care for our children, what options did other families have?

UNCERTAINTY, TRANSITIONS, AND AN UNEXPECTED OPPORTUNITY KATE SPENCE

Anxiety. Uncertainty. The university was on spring break the week leading up to the full shut down but my second and third graders were still attending our local elementary school in the metro New York City- New Jersey suburbs. And I wasn't sleeping. Did I have enough food? How could I possibly quarantine in our 1,500 sq. ft. apartment—we only have one bathroom and the CDC recommendations clearly stated anyone with COVID-19 should have their own bathroom … but who was I kidding anyway? There was no way my anxious 7-year-old would stop sneaking into my bed in the middle of the night during what was definitely the most uncertain time of his life. The single bathroom was not our biggest worry. So when the university announced that the two weeks following spring break would be conducted entirely online and then the kids' school district followed suit a few days later, I didn't hesitate. I didn't discuss it with their dad. I just decided. We were going to flee suburbia for the quiet, less populated countryside of VT, to hunker down with my mom and 88-year-old stepfather. My mom and stepdad were in the midst of a year-long downsizing process—they had sold the farm in October and were in a log cabin rental for a year while their new, smaller home was being built. The log cabin was situated on 35 acres of fields and forest, with a sometimes raging, other times babbling, brook. I packed 3 duffel bags with 2 weeks' worth of clothing, the kids' school backpacks, the books and plans I needed for my classes and of course, our winter gear. While spring had sprung in northern New Jersey, winter still held VT fully in its grasp. We left at 6am on Saturday morning, embarking on a 6-hour ride north. We arrived in a new climate with new, initially self-imposed restrictions: stay home, stay safe, stay hopeful. We quite literally did not leave the 35-acre log cabin homestead.

We quickly settled into a new routine. Most days I taught or had meetings during their traditional school hours, keeping up with my responsibilities as the director of our pre-service preparation program and teaching, but letting all delusions of research and publishing fall by the wayside. They're still there … by the wayside that is, as I continue to function as primary caretaker, virtual school facilitator, and professor. The boys learned how to feed the chickens and sheep, built snowmen and snow forts, and routinely fell into the brook, with these occurrences becoming less disastrous as they shed their snow pants and lined winter boots in favor of unlined mud boots and eventually, water-friendly sandals. Warmer weather brought with it fewer emergency loads in the dryer since their water-logged boots could simply be up-ended, water poured out, and set in the sun on the porch. They baked homemade cookies with Grammie-Nana and threw endless numbers of tennis balls for the border collie whose energy level rivals that of my 9-year-old. They were bored and simultaneously free in ways that only kids growing up in the country experience, relishing the ability to run out the door worry free, wander to the nearby recreation field, and complain bitterly that they weren't allowed to spend every waking moment plugged into their devices.

Until I finished my university commitments for the day and became their teacher, a transition we both came to dread. Though I was a teacher prior to moving into teacher education, I was a middle and high school English teacher. I specifically decided NOT to teach elementary school. And yet here we all were, embedded deeply in the juxtaposition between total country freedom and the rigidity of hours' worth of Google classroom, asynchronous assignments that for the most part, must have been lost in the void of the ether once the boys submitted them. The ferocity of their rejection of the synchronous "community-building" class meetings was shocking to me given all the suppositions educators were making about the isolation students were feeling. Perhaps it is my boys' commitment to expediency that led to them seeing these class meetings as a waste of their time, or the fact that they didn't think they were learning anything. We dutifully marched through endless tasks, listening to books online, watching animated instructional math videos, collecting, and upcycling materials into desk organizers, and secretly using the voice to text option to write their essays because what second and third grader can type proficiently? I forced compliance and completion in this part of their life, persisting through tears and frustration on both of our parts. We made it through only because of the grace of "flex Fridays," a day the district designated as a day for small-group intervention rather than new assignments and instruction. Internally, I tussled with the new uncertainty of what I should be prioritizing for their school experience. What would they gain or lose if they didn't complete the assignments that never received feedback anyway? Would I be able to transition back to a different reality where I did expect them to do what their teachers asked? It felt like a safer bet to stay the course, and persist through the stress. I'm still unsure.

Two weeks stretched into a month, then two, then three. Winter became spring became summer. We built campfires and roasted s'mores. We celebrated birthdays and holidays. We made reusable masks and shed tears about being isolated and the obvious inequities in our American society. We knelt on the statehouse lawn for George Floyd and protested in support of Black Lives Matter. We worried less and lived and loved in ways that were completely unexpected, building close ties with family.

And then we moved back, back to a new reality, with some of the same challenges we initially fled, but with masks this time, and slightly more manageable anxiety. Back to close quarters and suburban living. Back to fully remote school, at least in our district, as midway through the academic year the district hasn›t enacted the hybrid plan for K–12 schools yet. And continuing to tussle with uncertainty about learning: what works and why? What generalizations can be made from my boys' experiences, from my own teaching practices? And now that we're away from family again, how can we maintain the closeness this pandemic unexpectedly provided?

CHAPTER 32

UNCERTAINTY, TRANSITIONS, AND AN UNEXPECTED OPPORTUNITY

Kate Spence

Anxiety. Uncertainty. The university was on spring break the week leading up to the full shut down but my second and third graders were still attending our local elementary school in the metro New York City- New Jersey suburbs. And I wasn't sleeping. Did I have enough food? How could I possibly quarantine in our 1,500 sq. ft. apartment—we only have one bathroom and the CDC recommendations clearly stated anyone with COVID-19 should have their own bathroom ... but who was I kidding anyway? There was no way my anxious 7-year-old would stop sneaking into my bed in the middle of the night during what was definitely the most uncertain time of his life. The single bathroom was not our biggest worry. So when the university announced that the two weeks following spring break would be conducted entirely online and then the kids' school district followed suit a few days later, I didn't hesitate. I didn't discuss it with their dad. I just decided. We were going to flee suburbia for the quiet, less populated countryside of VT, to hunker down with my mom and 88-year-old stepfather. My mom and stepdad were in the midst of a year-long downsizing process—they had sold the farm in October and were in a log cabin rental for a year

Parenting in the Pandemic: The Collision of School, Work, and Life at Home, pp. 151–153
Copyright © 2021 by Information Age Publishing
151

while their new, smaller home was being built. The log cabin was situated on 35 acres of fields and forest, with a sometimes raging, other times babbling, brook. I packed 3 duffel bags with 2 weeks' worth of clothing, the kids' school backpacks, the books and plans I needed for my classes and of course, our winter gear. While spring had sprung in northern New Jersey, winter still held VT fully in its grasp. We left at 6am on Saturday morning, embarking on a 6-hour ride north. We arrived in a new climate with new, initially self-imposed restrictions: stay home, stay safe, stay hopeful. We quite literally did not leave the 35-acre log cabin homestead.

We quickly settled into a new routine. Most days I taught or had meetings during their traditional school hours, keeping up with my responsibilities as the director of our preservice preparation program and teaching, but letting all delusions of research and publishing fall by the wayside. They're still there ... by the wayside that is, as I continue to function as primary caretaker, virtual school facilitator, and professor. The boys learned how to feed the chickens and sheep, built snowmen and snow forts, and routinely fell into the brook, with these occurrences becoming less disastrous as they shed their snow pants and lined winter boots in favor of unlined mud boots and eventually, water-friendly sandals. Warmer weather brought with it fewer emergency loads in the dryer since their water-logged boots could simply be up-ended, water poured out, and set in the sun on the porch. They baked homemade cookies with Grammie-Nana and threw endless numbers of tennis balls for the border collie whose energy level rivals that of my 9-year-old. They were bored and simultaneously free in ways that only kids growing up in the country experience, relishing the ability to run out the door worry free, wander to the nearby recreation field, and complain bitterly that they weren't allowed to spend every waking moment plugged into their devices.

Until I finished my university commitments for the day and became their teacher, a transition we both came to dread. Though I was a teacher prior to moving into teacher education, I was a middle and high school English teacher. I specifically decided NOT to teach elementary school. And yet here we all were, embedded deeply in the juxtaposition between total country freedom and the rigidity of hours' worth of Google classroom, asynchronous assignments that for the most part, must have been lost in the void of the ether once the boys submitted them. The ferocity of their rejection of the synchronous "community-building" class meetings was shocking to me given all the suppositions educators were making about the isolation students were feeling. Perhaps it is my boys' commitment to expediency that led to them seeing these class meetings as a waste of their time, or the fact that they didn't think they were learning anything. We dutifully marched through endless tasks, listening to books online, watching animated instructional math videos, collecting and upcycling materials into desk organizers, and secretly using the voice to text option to write their essays because what second and third grader can type proficiently? I forced compliance and completion in this part of their life, persisting through tears and frustration on both of our parts. We made it through only because of the grace of "flex Fridays," a day the district designated as a day for small-group intervention rather than new assignments and instruction. Internally, I tussled with the new uncertainty of what I should be prioritizing for their school experience. What would they gain or lose if they didn't complete the assignments that never received feedback anyway? Would I be able to transition back to a different reality where I did expect them to do what their teachers asked? It felt like a safer bet to stay the course, and persist through the stress. I'm still unsure.

Two weeks stretched into a month, then two, then three. Winter became spring became summer. We built campfires and roasted s'mores. We celebrated birthdays and holidays. We made reusable masks and shed tears about being isolated and the obvious inequities in our American society. We knelt on the statehouse lawn for George Floyd and protested in support of Black Lives Matter. We worried less and lived and loved in ways that were completely unexpected, building close ties with family.

And then we moved back, back to a new reality, with some of the same challenges we initially fled, but with masks this time, and slightly more manageable anxiety. Back to close quarters and suburban living. Back to fully remote school, at least in our district, as midway through the academic year the district hasn›t enacted the hybrid plan for K–12 schools yet. And continuing to tussle with uncertainty about learning: what works and why? What generalizations can be made from my boys' experiences, from my own teaching practices? And now that we're away from family again, how can we maintain the closeness this pandemic unexpectedly provided?

CHAPTER 33

LIFE CAN BE HARD,
BUT IT IS BEAUTIFUL

Jing Lei

In mid-March, when schools were closed and students sent home, I was not too worried about my daughter's learning. Then a 7-year-old second grader, Arianna always loved school, loved learning, and had been doing very well without needing much help from me or her dad. Now learning from home, she had weekly packets of learning materials from school with daily schedule, so she should be able to follow the schedule and finish her daily work by mid-afternoon, and I could just focus on my work while she worked on her school assignments during the day.

Of course, it did not work out that way. The sudden outbreak of the pandemic threw the school and teachers off guard. The teachers were not prepared to teach online or even offer online help. As a matter of fact, teachers in the school district were expected to NOT offer any instruction online because not all students had access to online learning. As a result, Arianna worked on the new materials on her own, and she seemed to be doing well, reading, writing, and plugging away her learning packets. Or so I thought. Until about two weeks later when she was expected to return some of the work back to school. I went over her homework and found a number of places left blank, with sticky notes on which she had written,

Parenting in the Pandemic: The Collision of School, Work, and Life at Home, pp. 155–158
Copyright © 2021 by Information Age Publishing

"I don't understand" or "I need help."

I was not surprised that she had questions, but I was very surprised she didn't ask me to help. When I asked her why, she said: "Mommy, you are always busy. You had meetings all day long and you asked me to wait. I waited but then I forgot."

I felt very sorry and immensely guilty.

My little girl was trying her best to be a self-regulated and independent learner, doing as much as she could on her own. Yet when she needed help, her dear mom, a proud educator who had been very supportive and responsive to her students, did not provide timely assistance to the little learner in her own house!

What went wrong?

As I reflected on my work and life, I was forced to acknowledge the fact that I myself had been struggling silently since the shutdown. The pandemic had presented constant changes in our work that often needed to be addressed right away, which had in turn exacerbated the unprecedented challenges brought by the pandemic to everyone's life. As a professor and a department chair, I was not only the problem solver, but also a cheerleader for my colleagues, staff, and students during this very trying time. After a long day's meetings on various academic and administrative issues, I often found myself depleted of energy and drained of emotions, and thus too exhausted both physically and psychologically to be helpful to my own family. Working from home also meant work was never away from me. I was often lost in my thoughts over dinner or pondering about a work issue during a family conversation.

These yellow sticky notes were a wakeup call for me, and forced me to reevaluate my role as a mother/educator and to readjust my work/life balance (the lack of). I finally realized the reality that my daughter was learning without formal instruction, yet she didn't have the skills needed to learn on her own. She needed guidance to learn new materials, and she needed help to build the skills and habits necessary to become a successful independent learner. She also needed emotional and psychological support to help her navigate this new way of learning and living.

Another area that I realized she was missing was the social aspect of learning. One major reason she loved going to school was because she loved her teachers and classmates, and she even loved riding the school bus, chatting and having fun with her friends on the way. She missed her teachers, her classmates, her friends, school staff members, and the very kind school bus driver. For the first time, in her so-far rosy and happy little world, there was a real evil: The Corona Virus. She had many imaginary battles against the Corona Virus. She practiced her karate kicks and smacks very hard, hoping to chop down the virus so that she could go back to school. Children learn the best with their peers in social environments, but now that social interaction was taken away, and she had to explore, learn, ponder, stride or stumble, all on her own.

So, we adjusted our strategy, hoping to provide a more structured social learning environment, a "simulated schooling," for her. In the morning, after she got ready and had breakfast, she would go to "school," where her teacher Mrs. Mom or Mr. Dad (we had to take turns playing this role) would go over her agenda and plan for the day, then she would work on her school work alongside with the "teacher" (who would be doing their own work but available to help if needed). After "school" or on weekends, she had playdates with her friends, first virtual playdates on zoom or facetime, and later when the weather was good, outdoor social distancing playdates in parks. This "simulated schooling" kept her motivated in completing her school work in time, and gradually helped her build learning habits that could work for remote learning. After the fall semester started, her teachers finally provided online instructions every day, which was a great improvement for her learning, and most importantly, provided her opportunities for social interactions with her teachers and classmates.

To describe pandemic parenting, two words come to my mind. The first word is "interruption." I find myself frequently interrupted in the middle of writing, replying to an e-mail, trying to provide thoughtful and constructive feedback on student works, or even in the middle of a phone call or a zoom meeting. A friend forwarded me a study saying that the number of paper submissions by female researchers had decreased since the pandemic started. I was not surprised to hear that. As a researcher, what I cherish the most is focused time to engage in deep thinking and concentrate on my writing, but with constant interruptions from work and home, it is very difficult to be productive scholarly.

And the second word would be "conflicted." I often have conflicting thoughts and feelings, because I feel that in my role as a mother/educator, I am not doing a good job following the educational theories and principles that I have learned and believed in, or practicing the best practices in my education of my own child due to the lack of time and energy. At the beginning of the lockdown, like almost everyone else, I had turned to social networks to stay informed and connected. I have many parent friends. One parent lamented "I heard that people without children are taking over the world," and another parent described himself as "a mediocre employee, and a subpar parent." I laughed at their humor, and I shared their sense of worry and anxiety: am I doing a good job to help my child? And that anxiety is more acute since I'm an educator who is supposed to know the best theories and practices of educating a child, yet not meeting these expectations amongst my own struggles.

One Saturday afternoon in mid-October, I was taking Arianna to a park playdate with her best friend. She was so happy that she couldn't help from singing, and she was making up her own songs, singing what was in her mind, how excited she was, and what she saw outside of the car. Upstate New York in mid-October was as colorful and beautiful as a dreamland. As I drove through the stunning valleys and breathtaking hills, I heard she sang "Life can be hard, but it is beautiful!" I was surprised and amazed. I wondered what made an 8-year-old make such a sentimental claim about life being hard, and I was also amazed at the silver lining she added to the "hard life": it is beautiful! I looked at the rearview mirror and saw her sweet little face, full of happiness and excited anticipation of seeing her best friend soon. My eyes became misty.

Life can be hard, but it is beautiful! May your life always be beautiful!

CHAPTER 34

STRAIGHT OUTTA THE "CONTAINMENT ZONE"

Rosa L. Rivera-McCutchen

It was the afternoon of Tuesday, March 10, 2020. I had just finished up a weekly coaching call with a small group of untenured faculty, when I took my cell phone off of "do not disturb." I marveled absent-mindedly at the number of buzzing alerts that were popping up on my phone, when I opened up an e-mail from an advisee labeled "Thinking About You!," complete with an offer of a care package. Huh? I quickly opened up the *New York Times* website, and learned that part of my community had been declared a "Containment Zone," and Governor Andrew Cuomo was sending in the Army National Guard. Looking at the map of the now infamous "Containment Zone," I realized that the high school, where my husband teaches and where my eldest was in 10th grade, and one of the middle schools, where my 12-year-old was in the 7th grade, were included in the boundaries of this new zone. As I looked closer at the map, I realized that our home was just 3–4 houses just outside of the zone. My next thought was "CRAP!" This is how my experience with the pandemic began and, as it was for so many others, there was a mixture of fear and confusion. And, like others, my life was upended in what seemed like parallel universes: home and work, each of these with their own set of complex constellations.

Parenting in the Pandemic: The Collision of School, Work, and Life at Home, pp. 159–161

In my home "universe," four of the five members of my family were impacted by the closures in New Rochelle and my campus closing. My husband, a teacher at New Rochelle High School, and my two eldest had their schools closed. My youngest, then a 5th grader, attended an elementary school just outside of the "Containment Zone," and her school remained open for several more days until a district-wide closure went into effect.

As all of this was going on, I was also starting to feel sick. While I suspected that I had a simple cold because my body was run down from the stress of my child's hospitalization, I was concerned. Had the circumstances not been so grave, the quest to find a testing site could have been part of a comedy sketch. I was turned away at the first two locations, and as I was turned away from the third location, a Black woman working in the facility, likely sensing my increasing anxiety, reassured me in hushed tones that us Black folks didn't get this virus. After getting a tip from a friend that, despite requiring a prescription, the authorities were not turning people away at the newly opened drive-by testing facility, I raced over to get tested in a scene that eerily resembled the film "Contagion."

Going into quarantine with my family as we awaited my results (negative!), I was reminded time and time again of the importance of my "village." My colleagues and students all checked in on me with calls and e-mails. The other mothers in my community texted to see how we were doing, dropped off groceries, picked up prescriptions and delivered chicken soup. Despite the physical restrictions of the containment zone, my emotional connections to my community remained stronger than ever.

Meanwhile, in my parallel work universe, the month leading up to the day New Rochelle was placed in lockdown had felt utterly overwhelming after returning from my first sabbatical in the fall semester. I was teaching two sections of first year educational leadership certification students with whom I normally would have established rapport while teaching them in their first semester. Admissions season was just beginning to get underway, I was working on a critical accreditation report, and resuming a myriad of other responsibilities that colleagues had taken during my sabbatical. At the same time, I was stressed about not having written enough during the sabbatical. I had just started to feel as though I was getting into a groove, when we went into fully remote instruction.

Going into pandemic mode in both of my universes unsettled me to the core and I set out to make a plan for the few short weeks that our lives would be interrupted before returning to normal. I was struggling to keep up with the onslaught of Zoom meetings as well all attempted to figure out how we would proceed. The meetings started early and ended late into the evening. If there had been any semblance of work-life balance prior to the pandemic, it most certainly went out the window after we went into a lockdown. It was hard to refuse a meeting when everyone knew that you were home and available via Zoom. Besides, setting boundaries felt wrong when there were so many people I wanted to support: the faculty whom I supervise and our students, all of whom worked in schools and many with families of their own whose lives were also being disrupted. I preached grace, patience, and a reduction of stress, paying forward the support my community had extended to me.

At the same time, my own kids were at home, and every time I felt like I could exhale, I'd realize that my kids weren't having their needs met! The schools were still figuring out how to transition to "distance-learning" and the kids were not quite engaged in much. So, I posted a large piece of chart paper in the living room and enlisted my husband in coming up with a plan. When he told me that I was "on edge," I channeled every ounce of control to avoid cursing him out, and we proceeded to create a schedule that included exercise and documentary viewing every day. This grand plan lasted about 2 days.

For so long, I felt like I was constantly trying to keep everything at work and home in balance, trying to contain the chaos and fear. At some point though, I realized that containment was an illusion. Now, I work to lean into the here and now, and continue to turn to my community of friends, colleagues, and students to give and receive support.

CHAPTER 35

JUST THE TWO OF US

Solo Parenting During the Pandemic

Jessica Rigby

I'm a solo mama of a kiddo who turned 2 years old just as the pandemic settled in, and received news of my promotion to associate professor with tenure a few months before that. Unlike the experiences of many single moms during this time, our early pandemic journey is not a bad one, in part because of the stress release that tenure awarded me. Stay at home orders gave us the unusual gift of time with one another. We went on scavenger hunts, joined zoom music classes, cooked together, took the dog on endless walks, and had time to snuggle every morning. In many ways, it was joyful.

The two biggest challenges were finding space for myself and facing challenging decisions on my own, especially those with no good answer. The first I was able to maneuver around, and the second continues to weigh heavily.

I think it's important to begin with my racial and socioeconomic positionality: I'm White and own my home. Tenure gives me job security regardless of how much I don't publish this year. Coupled with an amazing housemate and a strong community of parents with kids of a similar age

Parenting in the Pandemic: The Collision of School, Work, and Life at Home, pp. 163–165
Copyright © 2021 by Information Age Publishing
All rights of reproduction in any form reserved.

to my daughter, solo parenting in the time of COVID and a national racial reckoning was not personally devastating, fearful, or lonely.

On space. Raising a toddler is not easy work; I hear about my friends who trade responsibilities with their partner, allowing each other space—to shower, go for a run, work, just be in their own heads. Typically, childcare gives me this space. During the first few months of COVID, our housemate, Katelynn (otherwise known as "Kay-tin") gave me this space. Katelynn moved in when I was trying to get pregnant via donor sperm and IVF. Nearly four years later, we refer to our living arrangement as Golden Girls 2020—we are good friends, support each other, make fun of each other, and take care of each other. COVID shut down the hair salon where she works and childcare for my daughter, but not my teaching duties. We arranged a childcare-for-rent trade that allowed me to work three mornings a week. This time was invaluable, not only because I was able to teach my class without my daughter on my lap, but because it allowed me some space for myself as a human, not only a mom.

In those early months, our small household podded up with another family who has a kid about the same age as my daughter. They were good friends before the pandemic; we often spent weekends together and went on impromptu walks and bike rides (they live about a 10-minute walk from my house). It became clear towards the end of February that the mom was going to lead a large international company's public health response to COVID. She worked about 90-hour weeks for the first four months of the pandemic. The dad, also a professor at my university, still had to teach and maintain his lab. Because I had the flexibility, I took care of both girls two mornings a week. After naptime, we'd walk over to their house, I'd get an hour or so to catch up on work, and we'd eat dinner together.

I remember thinking about the spring as a "bonus maternity leave" —I got to spend so much time with my daughter while still getting paid, and not expected to get a ton of work done. Similar to my maternity leave, I was expected to get *some* work done, but at least I was getting full nights of sleep and not nursing around the clock. Thinking back on those first couple of months in the spring, it was a really special time. My daughter and I spent hours together (instead of the quick mornings and evenings that are the status quo of the workweek), our family built a strong, lasting relationship with our pod family, we facetimed with my family everyday (mom, brothers, and their families), and our focus was narrowed to the basics of living. I had three work trips planned over those two months, and I wasn't unhappy with what I missed: all of the complications associated with work travel as a solo mom—finding care for my dog, care for my daughter on-site, a place for us to stay that met our needs, and six flights with a toddler. There was relief in the inability to do anything but go for walks, cook meals, and be with each other.

On decision making. It wasn't all relief, though. I woke up most nights worried about the work I wasn't getting done. When her childcare center opened up for nonessential workers on May 1st, I needed to make what seemed like the hardest decision I've had to make in her two short (longest ever) years. If I decided to keep her home, it was possible that I'd lose our spot until at least September. Katelynn was going back to work, so I couldn't rely on her for childcare. Was I willing to give up my work for four months? Was I able to give up my work for four months?

I knew that my daughter would be happier and better served by going back to school. She thrives there, energized by playing with many children, working with new tasks designed specifically for her developmental needs, and having an outdoor play space to run around. In May, we knew little about how COVID manifests in children or if childcare centers would become the new "superspreader" sites. I had the resources and flexibility to keep her home—and likely safer.

Was sending her back to childcare just selfish, putting us all at risk so that I could do work? Deep down in that decision was also a quiet but persistent wondering: is my work useful in the grand scheme of things? I don't save lives, I don't write policy. I'm a White lady arguing that we need to consider race in instructional leadership—something that BIPOC scholars and practitioners have long been experiencing, studying, and writing about. I know that I am not alone asking this question of the utility of my academic endeavors. This decision in a pandemic moment of isolation, heightened by a fear of sickness and death, coupled with the doubt around my work, amplified my solo-ness. It was an impossible dilemma with only bad outcomes, one that I wish I wasn't solely responsible for.

I sent her back, and perseverated for weeks before I let it go. As we start the new year, COVID cases are soaring and fear of the more contagious variant continues to keep me up at night. We had one 2-week childcare closure in the winter when one of the teachers' in my daughter's center was COVID positive. That time period didn't have the same openness in December that we had in March—my work demands were back to normal despite our continuing abnormal context, the dark and rainy winter of the Pacific Northwest enveloped us, and we both felt pandemic fatigue. Instead of scavenger hunts, we had Daniel Tiger. The molasses-paced vaccination rollout in our state (and nation) leaves me little hope for actual protection before September. Until then I expect that I'll continue to carry this weight and fear. I will also continually remind myself of my privilege, that which I am not carrying, and revel in the joy of what took years to come to fruition—motherhood itself.

CHAPTER 36

A STORY OF A PART-TIME PARENT DURING THE PANDEMIC

Bong Gee Jang

Me:	Should we continue sending him to his daycare or not?
My wife:	I don't know. If we have to.
Me:	"Have to?" What do you mean?
My wife:	I mean literally, if we have to … if there is no option, no choice, then we have to send him.
Me:	Do we have an option?
My wife:	Well…. We may or may not …

Feeling Guilty

I still cannot forget the above conversation that I had with my wife in mid-March. My son was one and a half years old at the time, and we had had him about 10 years after getting married. I had planned to seek tenure

Parenting in the Pandemic: The Collision of School, Work, and Life at Home, pp. 167–169
Copyright © 2021 by Information Age Publishing

and promotion during the following year, and my wife, a full-time nursing faculty member at another research-intensive institution, had just finished her mid-tenure evaluation and was preparing for a federal grant proposal. For about a week, we thought about whether we had any choice but to send him to daycare. I felt afraid after reading about the symptoms of children infected by COVID-19 as reported in newspapers. At the same time, I felt nervous about having limited time for my professional work. I felt guilty about considering continuing to send him to his daycare during the pandemic. We finally decided to keep him at home and to try to create flexible work schedules as much as possible.

Establishing New Daily Routines and Facing Struggles

My wife and I had to admit that we had been part-time parents (and full-time professionals) since we sent him to a daycare at six months old. My son spent most of his days (from 9 A.M. to 5 P.M.) at daycare on weekdays while we were working at our universities. Now that he was staying home, my wife and I split the day into two parts: from when he woke up in the morning (usually around 6:30 A.M.) until his nap (around 12:30 P.M.), and from after his nap (usually around 2:30 P.M.) until he went to bed in the evening (around 8 P.M.). I was in charge of the first shift, and my wife took care of him during the second shift. It was challenging—both physically and mentally—to take care of him (My respect for early childhood teachers has really grown!), and I often fell asleep with him during his nap. It seemed like a simple plan to focus on my work while my wife was taking care of him during the afternoon, but it was not easy to focus. My baby often called out "Daddy!" and came upstairs to my office to try to play peekaboo with me. Responding to e-mails was a priority, and preparing for online teaching, organizing virtual field placements, and giving feedback to students were secondary priorities. Although I had planned to spend at least 30 minutes per day writing, this proved almost impossible until the semester ended.

Slowing Down Instead of Finding a Balance

Since I started my career as an assistant professor, work/life balance was a key idea that I always kept in mind. I always dreamed of a perfect balance (50–50) on my work-and-life scale, with excellent quality on both sides. But during the pandemic, an effective balance became impossible. During the pandemic period, there has been no way to equally balance work and life with a young child at home, and my expectations for my quality of work and life shifted from "excellent" to "good enough." I thought it was a temporary, emergent condition due to COVID-19, but it soon became a new normal condition. I had to adjust to the new roles of a full-time parent, a fully online instructor, and a socially isolated individual. Everything felt new, and there was no time to practice. I slowed down my pace for both work and life and discarded the illusion of achieving balance.

Recognizing Opportunities Created

Slowing things down brings good and bad results. One of the bad aspects is that I don't get as much done; one of the good aspects is that I now see many little things that I did not notice before. For example, while taking care of my baby, I have observed his bilingual language development more closely. He has started to pronounce some basic words like "mommy" ("umma" in Korean) and "daddy" ("appa" in Korean) in both Korean and English. One interesting pattern I have observed repeatedly in his vocabulary development is that when it comes to choosing between English and Korean words with the same meaning, he usually picks the word with a phonetically simpler structure. For example, "fish" is a single-syllable word, and "moolgogi"—the Korean equivalent—has three syllables. Although we have taught him both words, he always opts for "fish" instead of "moolgogi." However, for "alligator," which has a much more complicated phonetic structure in English, he prefers the Korean word, "awk-uh," with fewer syllables. Slowing down has also meant that I read more picture books to him. Reading books together has allowed to me to observe similar examples.

Looking back to the days (has it really only been a year?) when my wife and I had the first conversation about whether to send our baby to daycare or keep him at home, it was an inevitable choice. Our decision was initially made from a place of both guilt and anxiety in this pandemic situation, and the consequences led to both new daily routines and mental and physical struggles. However, it was necessary for us to slow down and prioritize him. Not an easy task at all, but as we have shifted from part-time parents to full-time parents, we are now coming to appreciate joys and wonders that we were not able to recognize before.

CHAPTER 37

THE CHALLENGES AND GIFTS OF BEING A PARENT AND AN ACADEMIC IN A PANDEMIC

Carolyn Sattin-Bajaj

Fall quarter of 2020 waited for me like an exquisitely wrapped gift. With funds from a grant to launch a study of school leaders' responses to immigration enforcement threats and xenophobia, I had bought out my teaching obligations and planned to spend the quarter collecting data for the new study and finishing multiple writing projects. Finally, after two major transitions in two years—a yearlong sabbatical in Sydney, Australia followed by a move from Seton Hall University (in New Jersey) to the University of California, Santa Barbara the following year, by March 2020, my family had settled into our permanent home. Then, the pandemic hit.

With two children in elementary school (a kindergartener and third grader—both boys), my husband and I muddled through the final two and a half months of a sudden shift to virtual schooling to end the 2019–20 academic year. I quickly switched my two Spring courses to Zoom (both small seminars that adapted easily) and spent most of my days trying to keep the kids engaged in some semblance of academic work and extracurricular fun around the house. Our kindergartner boycotted the twice daily Zoom meetings entirely, but read the whole SpongeBob Squarepants early

Parenting in the Pandemic: The Collision of School, Work, and Life at Home, pp. 171–174

reader series to me. I took that as a win. Our third grader mastered his times tables and argued convincingly that playing Monopoly should count as practicing math if he was banker, a role he gladly assumed in the many hundreds of games we played before, during, and after school hours.

My husband and I knew how fortunate we were that neither of our children had learning needs that made homeschool additionally challenging for them (or us) and that our jobs allowed for the flexibility that was required to manage such a massive disruption to work, school, and life. Yet, we felt wholly unprepared for the task of helping our children through a drastic change in their schooling while attempting to meet our professional obligations. I, as a tenured professor in a graduate school of education and my husband, as a former public elementary school teacher who continues to work in the field of education policy, are seemingly among the most equipped to deal with these changes. Nevertheless, we had questions about what to reasonably demand from our children when they resisted participating in Zoom activities or finishing the 20th worksheet of the week. We knew less about what to expect from teachers during this unprecedented crisis in terms of academic rigor, engagement, and responsiveness to our children's (and our) needs. So, the entire family was thrilled and relieved when summer break started in early June, and we were released from the pressure of trying to do school from home.

Early summer messages from our school district indicating a likely in-person return were replaced by official declarations of indefinite virtual school after post-Memorial Day spikes in COVID-19 cases in California. Fall quarter of 2020 soon changed shape from a period of intensive research and writing to working as a full-time virtual teaching assistant for my children. Because we had moved into a new house mid-2020, the boys were starting at yet another new school—this time, virtually. So, despite my disappointment about not having nearly as much time to devote to my scholarly pursuits, I felt fortunate that I did not have to attempt to juggle Zoom teaching and overseeing their virtual learning while helping them navigate another new learning environment. I also naively thought that with three to four Zoom meetings per child daily, I would be able to squeeze in some emails and writing—a notion of which I was quickly disabused after the first week of constant interruptions—requests for technical support, for snacks, and for help finding the correct paper in the growing pile on the kitchen table.

What at first sparked frustration rapidly led to a sense of gratefulness: I felt grateful to have the opportunity to be a partner in my children's learning in a way I had never been before. I felt grateful to be able to enjoy time with my boys and fully dedicate myself to their virtual schooling without worrying about the consequences of not working an 8-hour day—both financially and in terms of the implications for a future tenure case.

Ultimately, we settled into a somewhat smooth flow on the schooling front. I've been incredibly impressed by the teachers' efforts to develop a sense of connection with students and among students whose relationships are mediated by screens, and I even see some real learning happening. (We've also moved from reading SpongeBob to National Geographic books, and I've never loved learning about snakes and lizards more!)

On the work front, I shifted my expectations and priorities in a way that helped reduce my anxiety about not being productive (in the typical sense). Instead of trying to finish six papers and engage in deep analytical thinking in the 3–4 hour window I have every afternoon to work (when my husband or a babysitter takes over or the boys participate in outdoor activities), I've decided to focus on small tasks that I can reasonably accomplish. This means agreeing to do more journal reviews than I ever have before, meeting (via Zoom) with prospective doctoral students interested in UCSB, reading drafts of students' or junior scholars' papers and grant applications, and participating in departmental service as a means to get to know my new colleagues and new department better, albeit from a distance. I also continue to supervise research assistants, and I have learned how to more effectively delegate tasks, which, under other circumstances, I may have taken on myself. These lessons about delegation have been mutually beneficial: students are taking on more analytic responsibility, which is important for their own development as researchers and my projects are moving forward without my intensive engagement.

Ultimately, I have been able to play an active role in my children's virtual schooling without feeling that I'm letting down my colleagues, coauthors, or students too much. This is a privilege that I do not take for granted. At the same time, the fact that I have been able to dial back my scholarly work so significantly with relatively few repercussions has raised some existential questions about the value of my work and my contributions to research, policy, or the greater good. I've also occasionally worried about the message my sons are receiving about gender roles and the importance of my professional life when it has been put on pause while my husband continues (by necessity) to work as much as or more than he did pre-pandemic (although without any of the demanding travel.)

In the end, I've tried to focus on the ways I have been able to contribute—to my family, my local community, my university, and the broader public. One professional highlight during this time was publishing a policy brief with the Annenberg Institute and Results for America through their EdReseach for Recovery series. Writing about research-based strategies to support students in immigrant families for an audience of district- and school leaders and policymakers, my coauthors and I felt like we were able to help people making difficult, time-sensitive decisions about how to meet students' needs during this time of unprecedented upheaval, at least in some small way. I shared the brief with some of the school districts in my local area, leading to a new invitation to work with local district administrators to use research to inform their equity and diversity planning and initiatives. These have served as welcome reminders about the potential for even minor investments of time or energy to have a positive impact.

While I am eager for the threat of COVID-19 to be eliminated and for life to return to "normal"—understanding that normal will likely look quite different from now on—this period has given me a chance to discover what I miss most about my professional life and what I want to be working on when it is possible to do so again. I've also found fulfillment in spending more of my time advancing other people's scholarship and focusing on work that might inform education policy and practice more directly. Pandemic parenting has profoundly influenced me as a scholar (and a mother): COVID-19 has reshaped the research questions I'm interested in and how I want to prioritize my time. It has also underscored for me the power of education research to inform evidenced-based practices in times of crisis. In the end, I have come to appreciate the insights gained through my experiences of pandemic parenting as an unexpected kind of gift wrapped in very different packaging.

CHAPTER 38

BLURRING OR ERASING THE LINES BETWEEN WORK AND HOME?

Raquel Muñiz

Since March 2020, when the COVID-19 pandemic caused a national shutdown, I have slowly made my own workspace at home, with a white board that resembles the one in my own office, a desk, a lamp, and even a second computer screen. I have also purchased the same pens as those in my office and set up a printing station next to my bookshelf. The transition was slow but steady—first a chair and a printer, then a table for the printer and a second screen, etc. The space has brought me comfort, giving me a piece of what life was like prior to the pandemic. I have transitioned my workspace home and have adapted my work in ways that are responsive to the pandemic. I have resorted to interviewing participants remotely via Zoom, the virtual video conference platform. I have sought ways to reconsider how to conduct observations via Zoom as well and have supplemented data through documents, to name a few changes. I meet with my research project collaborators and research team through a series of weekly Zoom meetings.

Still the ever-changing reality as a result of the pandemic is undeniable and shows up in stark ways. While the white board may have helpful quotes,

Parenting in the Pandemic: The Collision of School, Work, and Life at Home, pp. 175–177

conceptual maps, or bullet points with next steps for different projects, it also features the alphabet and other drawings my four-year-old has written and drawn when I have stepped away from my desk. Similarly, while a section of my desk includes drafts or articles, these are often buried under LEGO pieces, play food, drawings, and stories my four-year-old leaves me to brighten my days. When I leave my desk to grab a cup of coffee, I no longer walk down the hallways of Campion Hall, meeting and greeting students and colleagues, and my colleagues no longer greet me by the coffee machine where we commonly stopped to chat and catch up. And, when I meet with my students or teach in the evenings, it is not uncommon for my children to run into the room to share some news and find some time to talk. Amidst the pandemic, the lines between work and home have blurred, if not erased.

The pandemic has removed some of the lines that I had drawn and, what's worse, I have no manual to know how to navigate the discombobulation. None of us do. My office provided the much-needed silent space and uninterrupted time I needed to think through new ideas and arguments. I no longer have that space. Thus, I have to grapple with keeping up with the education literature, conducting research, giving talks, engaging with peers, and all other aspects of being an academic in the field of education, with knowing when to step away from work during "work hours" and attend to my children's needs. On any given day, I may be writing a paragraph on a manuscript and the next moment I am being asked to help with 11th grade mathematics homework, 10th grade writing homework, 6th grade speech class, and to sound out letters for my kindergartener who is learning how to spell and read amidst the pandemic.

As with many life-altering events, the pandemic has also shone light and provided perspective in many areas of my life. What truly matters in life? And for whom? I have seen family members and friends grapple with their mortality, some falling severely ill. Through conversations, they have contextualized what they see as important in life when their own mortality seems to be at issue. Suddenly, the upcoming deadline or meeting seems trivial. Through the conversations, I am reminded to appreciate the "small" things in life: for example, time spent with family walking neighborhood trails or playing board games, coffee and tea time with friends on Zoom, and being healthy and alive.

But this realization, as helpful and insightful as it has been, only complicates my ability to do that work from home; it has made juggling and prioritizing during the pandemic that much more difficult. I am often torn between continuing to edit, write, read, and analyze and, what feels like, continuing to build strong bonds with my children. When I am reading or writing and one of my children walks into the room to ask for help during one of their breaks from online learning, do I ask them to come back at a later time or do I drop what I am doing and ensure they know they are cared for and heard? The dilemma would not normally occur pre-pandemic, and now seems to have no easy resolutions—at least not for me as I try to reconsider what truly matters for me. I am not sure I will find a resolution soon or whether finding one should even be the goal. For now, I am seeking comfort in the moments when I have an opportunity to strengthen those relationships with my children and friends, as well as the moments of solitude when I can sit in relative silence to focus on my work, even as the lines have blurred or erased.

CHAPTER 39

TENURE TRACKING FROM HOME

Rachel Silver

My past ethnographic work has looked at the extraordinary efforts that student-mothers in Malawi make to go to school: the long, hot walks to and from class; the double, triple, quadruple daily shifts (farming/family/ schooling/family/studying); and the need to maintain rigid boundaries between their parenting and school-going selves. When at school, these young women could be students only. When at home, they were mothers first. The idea of a student mother was a contradiction in a deeply conservative policy landscape. (The same can be said, of course, in contexts across the world). I argued that these girls' ability to be in school relied on the separation of their identities as mothers and as students.

In my own life, I've been fortunate to erode the rigid barriers of identity to some extent. My PhD advisors were generous and feminist; one nursed through our meetings for years. I had my first baby as a graduate student and brought her with me on fieldwork. And, when I finished my doctorate and got a job, it was in Canada. I was granted parental leave even before I started teaching. What was a basic right to my faculty union was to me—and my peers in the U.S.—a massive, almost unbelievable, privilege.

I also weave my parenting self into my research and writing. An early section of my dissertation focuses on how being a mom shaped my work (as per disciplinary standards—an exercise in self reflexivity). Together

Parenting in the Pandemic: The Collision of School, Work, and Life at Home, pp. 179–181
Copyright © 2021 by Information Age Publishing
179

with a colleague, I organized a roundtable (cancelled, in the end) for the 2020 American Anthropological Association meeting on how parenting influences our epistemic viewpoints, fieldwork experiences, and knowledge production. My research looks explicitly at the confluence of sexuality, pregnancy, and education across space. I have spent the pandemic tracking the gendered treatment of risk in international development discourse, noting the disproportionate focus on sexuality for girls in the global South (e.g., fear of pregnancy) and on barriers to wellness in the global North (e.g., exclusion from sports).

Still, I came up in the same patriarchal academy as everyone else. I went on the job market, and to campus visits, hiding my second pregnancy (though perhaps not hiding it all that well). Once my son was born and my new job began, I brought him along. I wore him to my faculty orientation at six weeks old. I walked him around the department launch with my dean. My son nursed, napped, and bounced through the initial meetings with my tenure mentor, project codirector, and research officers. I worried what others thought, apologizing too many times. I told myself it was temporary. When leave was over, I would start my new job on a more "professional" footing. I would make a more serious impression, obscuring, if not erasing, the home/work divide.

As it turns out, I had 10 pre-pandemic weeks to do so. In that time, I did what so many academic parents do. I showed up at work, dressing formally, Medela® accoutrements in tow. I schlepped back and forth to campus, marking a physical separation between my two worlds (even if it was an artificial one, as I pumped at work and worked from home). I attended meetings on my own.

Despite being tired, I thought I was doing an okay job. I could stand in front of the class in big girl pants and not even mention my crawling baby or my daughter, now in her first year of kindergarten! I was there without my appendages, and no one knew I had been awake since 4:30 A.M.

Then COVID-19 struck. Boundaries collapsed on themselves, borders closed, and there I was—in my first ever semester on a tenure track job, trying to prove myself, teaching from my son's room with both kids in the house. My partner was a champ, and we did our best. We split hours, shuffling kids back and forth between us, trading work shifts promptly at 10:59 A.M. and again at 3:59 P.M. Still, I could no longer pretend to be "professional" in the way I thought was expected.

There was the introductory meeting with my first ever PhD student whose admission I had championed. During the call, my son shrieked so loudly I couldn't be heard while my daughter climbed a large stuffed deer toy behind me. Was the student stunned by his course requirements or by what his advisor was trying to pass off as a workspace? I got off the call and burst into tears. And then there was the orientation event for a research center I'm newly affiliated with. Faculty of all ranks came, including several big-name scholars whom I had yet to meet, as well as a host of graduate students. I logged on late, offering a profoundly incoherent introduction to my work over the sounds of our barking dog. "What did I even say?" I asked a colleague later. And there were the many, many meetings that went long when I thought to myself—these people clearly have more than three uninterrupted hours to work.

Still, many colleagues have been extraordinarily kind. They've shared their memories of raising kids in an academy with more patriarchy, if less pandemic. Some have learned my children's names and 'played' with them on screen. My daughter has made new friends in my department, chatting ice cream flavors, and showing off her drawings.

And, when this same sweet daughter surprised me during an evening graduate seminar with a "snack plate" she'd proudly assembled, my students—many of whom are parents themselves—smiled. That first PhD advisee was on the Zoom too. He said hello to my girl, and he waved enthusiastically. After all, we're in this together. And we're all exhausted.

Figure 39.1

School by Olivia (age 6)

CHAPTER 40

PANDEMIC PARENTING IN THE MIDDLE OF LIFE AND ACADEMIC TRANSITIONS

Diego Román

Even before COVID-19 hit the world, I knew that the 2019–2020 academic year was going to be filled with professional and personal uncertainties. At the professional level, after 5 years of teaching and conducting research in bilingual and science education at Southern Methodist University (SMU) in Dallas, Texas, I started a new position at the University of Wisconsin-Madison in July, 2019. Although I had enjoyed my position at SMU, I wanted to teach at a large R1 public institution located in the Midwest—a region that has experienced a rapid growth in its Latinx population. On the personal side, a year before this move, my ex-partner (Heidi) and I had gotten divorced. Heidi is from a town near Madison, where we both lived 15 years ago. So, moving back to Wisconsin meant for her to live near her parents again and that our 10-year-old son could grow up near his maternal grandparents—we had considered moving back to Wisconsin several times, but did not find the right time to do it. Thus, besides the great reputation of the university and its school of education, moving back to Madison seemed to be a good decision not only for my career, but also for my son and his mother. Yet, if moving to a new institution is never easy, doing so just before the COVID-19 pandemic hit the world added unforeseen complications to this transition.

Parenting in the Pandemic: The Collision of School, Work, and Life at Home, pp. 183–185
Copyright © 2021 by Information Age Publishing
All rights of reproduction in any form reserved.

My work examines the educational experiences and multilingual practices of Latinx students and families living in rural settings. Moving to Wisconsin has provided great opportunities to work with established and emerging Latinx communities living in various rural areas of the state. Since the beginning, my colleagues and students at UW-Madison have been extremely supportive and I was able to continue my research projects and teaching as soon as I arrived at Madison in the summer of 2019. My transition, in other words, started as smooth as possible. In relation to my personal life, Heidi and I have been able to maintain an amicable relation after our separation and have centered decisions that impacted our son considering what would be the most beneficial to him in the long run. I am truly thankful to her and I really appreciate that she was willing to discuss moving to Wisconsin, what this would mean for her professional career and personal life, as well as how I could stay close to my son.

Heidi only had some leads for jobs in Madison, but nothing concrete, when I started my position in Madison. For the time being, we decided that they will stay in Dallas and hope she could find a position in Wisconsin by the end of the 2019–2020 academic year, if at all possible. In that way, my son would finish fourth grade in Texas and start fifth grade in Wisconsin. In the meanwhile, our plan was that we will alternate visits; that is, I would fly to Dallas every other month and my son would fly to Madison the months in between. Our visits, however, came to an abrupt stop in February 2020, when the flight restrictions were put into place to contain the spread of the pandemic. Moreover, we did not know whether he or I should visit. Had I, for instance, been exposed to the virus and will visiting put my son and his mother at risk? We also talked about various scenarios. What if Heidi got sick in Dallas? Who would take care of her and our son? Her parents are older, and we did not want to expose them, and all my family is in Ecuador, where I am from originally. Also, and even though instruction went to a virtual format for my son and for my courses, we did not know if face-to-face instruction was going to resume any time soon. We decided to take one day at a time and that if needed, I would drive to Dallas and stay with them.

In the middle of all these personal decisions, a doctoral seminar I was teaching during the Spring semester addressing the linguistic practices of multilingual communities was moved to an online format following the policies adopted by the university. All instructors had to adapt the remaining semester sessions to synchronous or asynchronous instruction to accommodate our students' access to technology as well as the constraints they were facing in their personal lives. In my case, I decided to mostly conduct asynchronous sessions by creating modules for each class that had a variety of interactive activities using podcasts, Kaltura quizzes, and readings and discussion boards using Canvas. We met synchronously as a group via Zoom, as needed, and I had weekly meetings with students who were presenting their work each class. Given the topic of my course, I had many international students as well as some who came from minoritized communities in the United States. I believe that having asynchronous instruction helped at that time as I was not sure what was happening in my students' lives. Yet, not having face-to-face meetings with students completely changed the type of instruction I was used to conducting. I have always thought of myself as an effective in-person instructor but did not know how engaging my course would be in an online format, particularly given the sudden transition to a virtual environment. I can only say that I did my best considering the circumstances and my students have mentioned that they were grateful for the way the course was adapted.

My son and I stayed in contact only virtually from February to late May 2020. When his academic year ended Heidi and I decided to drive and meet half-way in Springfield, Missouri, which we discovered is located about 8 hours by car from both Madison and from Dallas. We did this a couple of times during the summer and my son ended up staying with me for half the summer months. He was also able to visit his maternal grandparents after we were sure we were not infected. Thankfully, Heidi was able to find a job in Madison and she and my son moved here permanently in August. Being near him/them has made an incredible difference for all of us. In fact, I believe that the one of the most important things the COVID-19 pandemic has taught us is the importance of being near loved ones, particularly as changes, some unexpected and some not, happen in our lives.

Figure 40.1

Visiting Papi by Andres (age 11)

CHAPTER 41

SINKING AND SWIMMING THROUGH THE COVID-19 PANDEMIC

Kristen Bottema-Beutel

It is difficult to settle on a framework for writing this essay. On the one hand, I find it cathartic to have a forum to express how difficult the past ten months of pandemic life have been for me and my family of five. After all, we have been in our house, together, all day every day since March 2020. We have not, however, lost a family member, our livelihoods, or our home, which leaves us much to be grateful for. I also have a partner—so I am not one of the many people parenting alone, and tenure—making my job more stable, and perhaps allowing me to speak a bit more freely about my experiences without fear of repercussions. Neither of my two school age children receive special education services, so they have been able to access and adapt to online learning in ways that might not be possible for many students. Although we are certainly not the family whose story is most in need of attention, I will take this opportunity to outline what our lives have been like, the shortcomings of the institutions we had hoped would support us, and the unanticipated ways we have changed.

My husband, Dave, is a high school teacher, I am an associate professor in a school of education, and our three children are 9, 7, and 11 months.

Parenting in the Pandemic: The Collision of School, Work, and Life at Home, pp. 187–189
Copyright © 2021 by Information Age Publishing

Dave teaches online, I do my research and teaching online, and the two older kids are in a Boston Public School learning online five days a week. Like many families with an academic parent, we do not live near our family, and so do not have help from aunts, uncles, or grandparents. Initially, Dave and I shared baby wrangling duties while we tried to rack up productivity hours that approached a full work day. About two months ago we hired a part time nanny which has made our lives much easier; and also made even starker the privilege we experience in comparison to our community members who have been unable to find any childcare. In Boston, childcare for children under three was hard to come by before the pandemic, and is nearly impossible to find now. Even with help, Dave's students greet the baby at least once a week as he teaches with the baby on his lap, and a good number of my fellow faculty have helped my 7-year-old with whatever task he's been given for a stretch of asynchronous learning ("I need five words that rhyme with think!" "How do I draw something that represents the word 'accessible'"??). My 9-year old is the most independent in terms of her ability to navigate a day of online school, but the isolation has been hard for her. Several times a week she needs a joint workspace—usually in my office—to lift her out of the doldrums.

Pandemic parenting, when childcare is scarce and expensive, has revealed how little academic institutions are prepared to assess, understand, and help faculty with childcare needs. While I have received e-mails of concern from department-level colleagues, there has been no significant attempts by upper-level administration—where policies are actually made—to assist parents who are without childcare. If you find this situation ironic given that I am employed in a school of education, you are in good company. Certainly, administration is aware that public schools are closed, requiring parents to, at a minimum, be home while their children learn online. Despite this, my university maintains an "accommodation request" process, which requires faculty to make a medical case for needing to work from home. Having children at home is not listed as an acceptable reason for granting an accommodation. Because I am tenured and teach graduate courses, where the push for in-person learning is significantly less than undergraduate courses, I will be teaching online anyway. But what about untenured faculty? Adjunct faculty? Graduate student teaching fellows? And even if I am able to work from home, how do I actually do that with three children and minimal help?

My husband's experience has been similar. Just yesterday, he received an e-mail from his superintendent indicating that he will be expected to teach in-person four days a week starting in January (he does not teach in the district where my children attend school, which will remain closed). As luck would have it, our part-time nanny is also leaving to attend college in-person starting in late January, and I will go back to teaching my full course load. My husband's school district has addressed the childcare crisis that has been a problem for many Bostonians—if childcare is an issue, simply take an unpaid leave of absence. This is, of course, impossible for us; we simply cannot take the financial hit of losing my husband's income. So, after 10 months of barely managing, we will increase our work responsibilities as I return to teaching, while what little childcare we had will evaporate. Institutional accommodations—such as flexible teaching options (e.g., teaching online) or expansions of on-campus childcare offerings (e.g., which currently only accept children who are between 2.9 and 5 years old) would have helped, but as far as I can tell there has been no serious discussion of these options.

Even as our situation becomes more untenable, there are ways that my family has grown and learned this year. My youngest will have lived his first year surrounded by his family, a state of affairs hard to come by in the U.S. with minimal paid maternity leave. He learned to sit, crawl, stand, walk, and say his first words ("Oh!" and "Wow!") with all four of us watching. My two older children are now closer than before the pandemic and rely on each other more now than ever for comfort, help, and companionship. Because of their dedicated teachers, they can now navigate online spaces— both social and academic—in ways that have enriched their lives. They have also learned critical lessons about the world around them: the realities of medical racism and privilege, the fragile state of our government, the lie of American exceptionalism, the social responsibility to protect your community from an unseen virus. An especially hard lesson for my husband and I is learning that supporting parents and other care-providers is an afterthought for most institutions, even those that have children at the center of their missions.

CHAPTER 42

THE THINGS I LEARNED

Katharine O. Strunk

In the before-times, before the onset of a global pandemic, my schedule was so tight that if one thing went wrong in a day—if a kid was sick and needed to be picked up from school or if my car got a flat and I needed to take it in to get replaced or if a sitter couldn't make it that afternoon—all the intertwined pieces of the day and week I had planned out so carefully would fall apart like a house of cards. I remember—and even though it was just a year ago, it feels like a decade—I remember thinking that there was no time to do it all. That I could not manage to be both an academic and a mother, a researcher and a wife, a teacher, and a friend. In the before-times, I felt like everything was so delicately balanced and one stray breeze would topple over the whole darn thing.

And then on March 13, 2020 the house of cards came crashing down. Suddenly my whole family was working from home. My kids—8-year-old twin boys in the second grade—not only didn't have in-person schooling, but for the first many weeks didn't have *any* schooling whatsoever. On top of all that, one of my sons had been diagnosed with ADHD and dyslexia eight months earlier and we had finally gotten him on a schedule with in- and out-of-school interventions. He had just a few months earlier turned a corner and was making great progress. And all of it—all of the carefully laid plans and tetris-like fitting of calendars and schedules together—vanished.

Parenting in the Pandemic: The Collision of School, Work, and Life at Home, pp. 191–194
Copyright © 2021 by Information Age Publishing

The early days of the pandemic were both frenzied and strangely calm. For the first time since my children were born, I consistently spent four or five hours a day with them, helping them with their school work and teaching them the skills and content that they would have been learning had they been in school. Luckily, I have a husband who shares the parenting load equally with me. Although this *should* be the norm rather than the exception, it isn't, which has been evidenced by the extraordinary toll the pandemic has taken on working mothers' careers and health. We set up a strict home-schooling schedule, each taking the kids for half of the school day. We built models of the heart and learned how it beats and read stories about maps and made paper-mache globes. We covered suffixes and prefixes and taught them how to write argumentative essays. Sometimes they loved it and us for trying so hard, and sometimes they lashed out and told us that they missed their "real teachers" and their friends. And yet somehow the homeschooling schedule became the thing giving all of us structure in our days and weeks and we all held on to it for dear life.

My other waking hours were spent attempting to get all the work done that I would normally do in a day—meeting with students and postdocs and colleagues at strange hours of the morning and night. I'd finish my own work at midnight and then stay up another hour pulling together the next day's second grade lesson plan. Weekdays merged with weekends and work time melded with home time and slowly I lost track of when I was professoring and when I was mothering and all of it became simply existing.

It might have made sense to step back and decide that I could set aside some of my work for a while. Many of my colleagues quite understandably did so. However instead I took on more work. In addition to the projects, I was running and the reports and papers I was writing with my team of amazing and committed research staff, graduate assistants, and postdocs, my team and I began to shift our research agenda to better understand how the pandemic was affecting students and educators. We fielded surveys and coded learning plans and turned around analyses faster than we ever had before. We presented to stakeholders and policymakers in an attempt to bring evidence into the conversation about the effects of the pandemic on public schools, educators, and students. It became almost an insatiable need to learn more about what was happening around us, to try to document the inequities facing our students, to try to advocate for the system of public education in which we so firmly believe. As it felt like everything was unraveling around us, our shared commitment to documenting and understanding and uncovering what was happening to public school students and educators gave us a sense of purpose, a feeling that we could contribute and help in some small way.

Based on the quantity of papers and reports being produced by researchers around the country on the topic of COVID and education, it is clear that

I was not alone in feeling the need to do something. And as researchers, what we know how to do best is research and document and analyze. And what did I learn?

I learned things about our public education system that reinforced and expanded upon what I already knew. The U.S. system of public education continues to serve some kids far better than others and these disparities are inexorably tied to race, ethnicity, income, and geography. A global pandemic is not a great equalizer but rather something that cements disparities and inequities and will have implications for years to come. Educators care deeply about their students—often more than they care about themselves—and their concerns run deep and wide. Politics more than evidence dictates education policy, even when stakeholders are trying their best to do the right thing for kids and educators.

I learned things about myself, things that I also already knew. When the world is chaotic and things feel out of control, I am a person who manages by managing. I am not one who can sit still and even when there is nothing that can be done I need to try to do something. When things are scary and uncertain I crave facts and evidence and I have faith that with that evidence we can affect some change—no matter how small.

I learned things about my own children. I began to understand how they comprehend and how they think in a classroom and their fears and insecurities and the things that they are proud of and the ways their eyes shine when they finally understand a concept or an idea. I witnessed their love of reading grow as they devoured the entire Harry Potter series and turned to whatever fantastic book I could find for them next. I watched as my son with dyslexia wrote complicated stories about dogs and friends and began to overcome his fear of spelling something incorrectly.

I saw that my children are caring human beings who want to take care of their parents as much as their parents want to take care of them. They showed us this in large and small ways, like when they surprised my husband and me with a fancy dinner of hamburgers and cookies which they served wearing the dressiest clothes they could find.

I learned that my kids understand more than we thought they did about the way the world works and the way we exist in the world. They listened quietly to the news reports about the increasing death toll from COVID and asked if they could write letters to loved ones. We talked about the growing racial unrest in our country and what it meant, and they asked if we could support the protesters and put signs up in the front yard.

Maybe most importantly, I learned that there is space to be both an academic and a parent, even when it feels like there is not enough time or energy to be both. Doing all the things is a privilege and a gift we are given. It is a choice we make. I like to think that I will take that lesson with me once we enter the after-times, when the world has returned to its normal pace and we begin the long road to recovery. I like to think that even when we go back to a time when schedules fit together like tetris pieces, I will know that I can be both an academic and a mother, a researcher and a wife, a teacher, and a friend.

CHAPTER 43

TENURED PROFESSOR, NOVICE PARENT

A Pandemic Tale of Love and Learning

Melissa A. Martinez

I've been an educator for almost 20 years; taught and loved other peoples' elementary aged children as my own as a teacher and counselor, then continued to facilitate learning for adults in educational leadership preparation. I don't have biological children of my own, so my role as a parent, in caring for children, had been limited to my experience as an educator and as an aunt to my two nieces and one nephew up until 2017. It was then that at the age of 39, I married my partner, who has a son from a previous marriage. I didn't get to meet my stepson, or "bonus" son in person until 2018, as he was only 6 years old then and lived in Florida with his mom. Since then, we've been able to have our son with us in Austin, TX for holidays and during the summer. Over the course of these visits and given the long distance between us, there's been a lot of learning and adjusting for our family of three, and particularly on my part as a stepmom; figuring out and respecting the boundaries of my role, working to build a solid, respectful and loving relationship with my now 8-year-old stepson while also reconciling my ideals and realistic practices of parenthood with those of my partner.

Parenting in the Pandemic: The Collision of School, Work, and Life at Home, pp. 195–197

When the pandemic hit in March of 2020, my role as a stepmom, my experience as a teacher, and the privilege I have in being a tenured professor in educational leadership with a flexible schedule came to a head. As schools began to shut down across the country my stepson was able to complete his school work from home. With his mother needing to work full-time, and his aging, Spanish speaking grandmother being the only one at home to assist him with his online schooling it became apparent that his Texas family needed to step in to provide more support. We gladly made the close to 20-hour drive to Florida in early May so he could finish out second grade in Austin and stay with us until August before he'd return to Florida, when we hoped the pandemic would be under control.

Fast forward and lots happened in between. We got through second grade, but the reality was that spring was such a turmoil for educators that the online schooling we were helping our son complete was mostly asynchronous and consisted of assignments that weren't difficult for him to complete on his own. The real challenge came in fall 2020 once educators were more equipped and able to require synchronous and asynchronous participation and assignments. Though my stepson started off third grade physically in Florida, by October his mom reached out; knowing we could provide more academic support given my being an educator and fluent in English—his mom and my husband are both predominant Spanish speakers originally from Venezuela. And though I was excited about having our son with us for the rest of the fall semester—which felt more like real life and not a holiday—I don't think I realized just how hard it would be.

By late October, I was juggling online teaching amidst the chronic stress of the pandemic and ongoing political and racial turmoil in our country, while grieving the loss of my father who passed away in late September, and taking on the full-time role as a stepmom. As a professor, I tried to be as supportive and flexible as possible with my educational leadership students and doctoral advisees. They were similarly trying to stay sane amidst rapidly changing district mandates requiring some to teach and lead from home, some fully online and some in hybrid formats all while managing their own familial obligations. Some, like me, lost loved ones in the fall to the pandemic and to natural causes; the uncertainty and loss just seemed to be a constant. The anxiety and fear was palpable at times, in their voices and on their faces, and I'm sure in mine too. Though together we managed to forge a community online, and I gave grace and asked for much grace from them through it all. I also tried to be patient with myself, especially as my love of and will to write and engage in research was at an all-time low.

Meanwhile, as I was the "official" teacher in the house, my husband deferred to me in helping guide and support our son with schooling. It took me at least a week before I learned his schedule and could navigate all of the different applications he had to use to complete his assignments:

Clever to log in; Canvas to house all the applications and some assignments; Microsoft Teams to log onto his three synchronous class meetings everyday—an hour earlier in Texas because of the time difference—Reading Plus; iReady; Think Central for Math; Imagine Math; Suite 360 for social studies; and Stemscopes for science. After the first week though, we all settled into our fast-paced routine. Mondays began with me printing out the agenda with the week's assignments for my son. He then had breakfast every morning by 6:30 a.m., the first synchronous class from 7:00-8:00 am, followed by Reading and Language arts independent assignments, the second synchronous class from 9:30–10:15 A.M., with independent math to follow. Lunch break was next, followed by his last synchronous class session from 11:20 A.M.–12:00 P.M. He'd finish social studies or science, plus anything else that hadn't been finished after that. Whoooo ... if it sounds like a lot. It is.

Here we were, two parents with degrees and flexible schedules, and we were struggling to keep up with both the content and number of assignments our son had while keeping him motivated with this online format. All I kept thinking was, how are less fortunate parents supposed to do this? There are parents who have to work full-time but would prefer to have their kids learning virtually, single parents, recent immigrant parents, non-English speaking parents, folks with slow or no internet or limited technological skills; not to mention students with special needs. And while I know teachers and school leaders are doing the best they can, the inequities within our K–12 education system that I'm all too familiar with through my research, became only more evident than ever via pandemic parenting and schooling.

Yet despite any challenges that came with parenting during a pandemic, I am extremely grateful for the love and learning that has come out of this experience. I may have three degrees and be a tenured professor of education, but none of those degrees or experiences truly prepared me for this. The joy of seeing my son learn new concepts in math and science that he never knew; feeling proud that he'd improved 2 levels in reading since last year; getting to know him as a little person and budding artist who loves sketching anime. Then helping him learn to navigate his feelings of frustration when he didn't understand something; offering *consejos* to shed light on why school and learning is important; and wiping away tears when he had the occasional meltdown because he would rather be playing outside or watching tv than having to answer reading comprehension questions for stories he didn't always find relevant to his life. I don't regret any of the professional sacrifices I have made and will continue to make with this new parenting role I've embraced. All of this to say, that despite the great losses that came with and during the pandemic, there has been much more gained in love, patience, and grace than ever before.

CHAPTER 44

PROFESSOR/PARENT

Corrie Stone-Johnson

Professor. Parent. Two halves of a whole. For most of my academic career I have tried to keep these identities in balance, to maintain a sense of homeostasis. If the two halves add up to a whole, though, I cannot do both roles well. More of one means less of another. In the pre-tenure days, the balance was near impossible to maintain. I began my academic job when my children were two and four. For days, I would hide away in my home office or at the university, writing papers and grading papers while my children grew. The best days—and also the worst days—were when my partner would take the kids away for the weekend. More professor. Less parent. They went hiking in the White Mountains in New Hampshire while I finished my book. They went to Ithaca to see the gorges while I prepared classes. More time for work. Less time for fun.

As the years ticked by my work as a professor and a parent began to stabilize. My children grew. Their needs shifted. My needs shifted. Their independence and social growth required that I spend less, not more, time with them. They went to camps for the summer. My days were free. I could focus more on my role as a professor, but at the same time it felt as though my role as a parent was shifting. I suddenly had more time to work, but with a surprising sadness in doing so.

_____

Parenting in the Pandemic: The Collision of School, Work, and Life at Home, pp. 199–201

March 2020 came in like a lion but never left like the proverbial lamb. We were frozen like our Zoom screens. Independence and social lives vaporized into the wind. Home was work. Work was home. No boundaries, only blurry lines. The internet crashed under the pressure of too many logins. Our faces froze on our tiny screens. We forgot to unmute. We turned off our cameras rather than pretend that life was normal.

My children, now teenagers, are older, more independent. They did their classes on their own. As a scholar who focuses on the power of relationships, I watched as my children struggled with the loss of in-person interaction. At the same time, we could not hold anyone responsible for the lack of academic rigor. Teachers held on by a thread, their own children on their laps and in their backgrounds as they attempted to make polynomials and grammar meaningful. I also research and teach educational leadership, yet I sat idly by as I saw our school leader retreat into silence.

My children raged against the injustices of the world, but from inside, behind closed doors. The protests of the spring were seen from a distance. Two of us suffer from chronic illnesses that made fear of COVID dominate our lives. Too much danger if we went. We stayed at the fringes.

My daughter, an eighth grader, missed out on the transitional rituals between middle and high school. No graduation. No parties. My son, a sixth grader, grew two shoe sizes, but it did not matter as he did not need shoes anymore. His real life and his video game life were barely discernible from one another. Every parental norm fell away. No screen limits. Real Pop Tarts from the grocery store. Breakfast for dinner. Guilt set in. Our home lives and Zoom lives were indiscernible, wholes divided into squares, everyone in their own space. We felt more than ever the privilege of our lives while the rest of the world sickened and fell away.

School gave up, swapping a full day of lessons for 45-minute well-being check-ins and then ending altogether. Summer camp was canceled. Work, however, was not. Summer courses needed to be taught, online. Fall courses needed to be converted. Student recruitment for academic programs needed to ramp up with fears that enrollment would tank. Students needed extensions. Dissertations came due. Colleagues needed support. Editors wanted papers reviewed. More work. Less parent. I was not the parent I wanted to be. I was not the professor I wanted to be. I barely was anything at all.

Throughout the last year, I have continually reflected on the tension that grows between being a professor and a parent. I have a brilliant colleague who writes about work-family balance and whose scholarship describes the ideal worker. The ideal worker works as though there are no other demands on their time (Sallee, 2012). Ideal, however, is defined not by the worker but by the work. It is not my ideal. But if I am an ideal worker, working without an eye toward my other obligations, I cannot be an ideal parent. One can only be ideal in one realm. One has to be either/or. Professor or parent.

There is a particular melancholy in parenting teenagers. The less they need you, the more you need them. One can no longer be an ideal parent, parenting as though there are no other demands on one's time, because there is no longer the same need. The children define the role. Theoretically, this shift would allow a person who lives in parent/professor limbo to become the ideal worker. As a professor, it could be argued that this is the perfect arrangement. All that time that used to be spent parenting is finally free, available to be dedicated to work. But the expected freedom does not feel as though it has materialized. What remains is a sense of loss, truly. COVID has only exacerbated this tension, upsetting the balance again between professor and parent. I am home more but needed less. Work needs me more but I want to be there less. Homeostasis was an only illusion, in the end.

The professor/parent balance might not be achievable. Rather, the extended quarantine has allowed for some needed reflection on what the ideal could or should look like, at least for me. It has truly been a privilege to stay home during these months. The job that at times felt like it defined every aspect of my life also allowed me to work from home alongside my children. While there may never be balance, there is a palpable sense of peace for the moment. From my desk in the attic I can hear a saxophone being played, a child laughing in a class meeting. I can eat lunch with my children and hear about their days in a way that I could not before. I also get to see what they are like as students, something I never would see otherwise. I hear how they talk in class, how they joke with a teacher. Maybe what seemed like being needed less is actually simply being needed differently. In the end, I will miss this time being at home with them. Perhaps balance is actually not equal work in both realms but rather a sense of peace in figuring out how to navigate the dual roles of professor and parent as an ongoing research project, a longitudinal study in modern work/life where the process of discovery matters nearly as much as the findings.

REFERENCE

Sallee, M. W. (2012). The ideal worker or the ideal father: Organizational structures and culture in the gendered university. *Research in Higher Education*, *53*(7), 782–802.

A FINAL NOTE
TO OUR READERS

At the time of this publishing, we are a year into the pandemic. Last March, we watched the world screech to a halt as schools, universities, and entire cities shut down. In our isolation, we hoped the pandemic would be short-lived and that we would soon resume our daily lives. As time has passed, we are still living with uncertainty and disruption. Over the course of this year, we have experienced the range of emotions, all within the microcosm of our own homes and families.

For us, the project came from a desire to create a communal space for sharing our experiences and to remind ourselves and one another that we are not alone in these struggles. Many of us are looking for ways to honor ourselves and our commitments, even as we quarantine. We are reinventing schooling at home and seeking balance between work and parenting. As the days blur together, we also sought to make a historical record, to document our daily lives in the pandemic.

Our hope is that this book brings us together and that we find comfort and connection in our shared experiences. With the help of friends and colleagues with a wide range of experiences, we have compiled a powerful set of stories that serve to build community as we continue to parent in the pandemic. Reading these stories has helped us reflect on our own experiences and discover new perspectives about our shared circumstances. The

Parenting in the Pandemic: The Collision of School, Work, and Life at Home, pp. 203–204
Copyright © 2021 by Information Age Publishing

writing carries us into the homes of the authors in new and personal ways. As professors pre-pandemic, we might not have brought our parenting into the workplace. In the pandemic, home is the site for both, and these stories illustrate our whole lives in ways we often don't share with each other. The personal and professional collide and we wear our multiple roles on our sleeves. It is our hope that by sharing these weighty, personal stories, we all feel a little less alone.

Hopefully, we will be out of this particular challenge, this pandemic, soon, and we will turn our attention to imagining life after. Then, and even now, we hope to continue to draw on our collective experiences for strength, wisdom, and resilience.

Sincerely,

Becca and George

ABOUT THE AUTHORS

William R. Black is a Professor of Educational Leadership and Policy Studies at the University of South Florida and daddy to Gabriel and David. He is the coeditor of the *Research and Theory in Educational Administration* book series and former coeditor of the *Journal of Cases in Educational Leadership*. His research interests include school leadership preparation and partnerships, as well as educational policy implementation, with emphasis disability and bilingual/bicultural education. He is glad 2020 is over and looks forward to his leadership work with the University Council for Educational Administration in 2021. He may be reached at wrblack@usf.edu.

Joshua Bornstein is an Assistant Professor and Director of Educational Leadership at Fairleigh Dickinson University. Dr. Bornstein has served as teacher, union leader, principal, staff developer, and school board member. He has worked in urban, rural, and suburban communities in Maryland, New Jersey, and New York. Dr. Bornstein's case studies on disrupting ableism and white supremacy can be found in *Journal of Case Studies in Educational Leadership, Review of Disability Studies, The SoJo Journal of Educational Foundations and Social Justice Education,* and the *Journal of Ethnographic and Qualitative Research.*

Kristen Bottema-Beutel is an associate professor of special education in the Lynch School of Education and Human Development at Boston College. She conducts research and teaching related to autistic children, youth, and adults. Specifically, her research has examined autistic social interaction, social development, classroom engagement, and has critically evaluated intervention literature. She lives in Boston with her husband and three children.

Vincent Cho is an Associate Professor in educational leadership at Boston College. A former teacher and administrator, his research addresses issues relating to school leadership in the digital age. Recent projects have examined administrators' uses of social media, 1:1 computing initiatives, and educators' uses of academic and behavioral information systems.

Elisa Macedo Dekaney is Professor of Music Education in the School of Education and the College of the Visual and Performing Arts (VPA) at Syracuse University. She currently serves as Associate Dean for Research, Graduate Studies, and Internationalization for VPA. Born in Rio de Janeiro, Brazil, has been an active researcher, clinician, and choral conductor in the United States and abroad. Her scholarly research focuses on aesthetic response to Brazilian music, choral repertoire from the global community, International Phonetic Alphabet, clinical simulation, and the intersection of music, race, and food. She is mother to Lucas, a freshman in college, and Nicholas, an eleventh grader.

Lisa M. Dorner is an Associate Professor and Cambio Center Fellow at the University of Missouri-Columbia: a teacher, researcher, and life-long learner; a lover of language, intercultural connection, and the idea of educación—including for her own two teenagers. Her work falls into three main areas: the politics/planning of bilingual education, educational policy implementation, and immigrant family integration in "new" spaces like rural Missouri. She is especially interested in the development of language immersion education, how immigrant families and children navigate educational options, and how to fight for equity in multilingual spaces. Lisa's work can be found in the *American Educational Research Journal, Educational Policy, Journal of Language, Identity and Education*, and *TESOL Quarterly*. Her website is lisamdorner.com.

Sharon Dotger is a spouse and mother of two daughters. She is a science teacher educator and a lesson study practitioner/researcher. She enjoys exercise and quilting.

Shaun M. Dougherty is an Associate Professor of Public Policy & Education at Vanderbilt University's Peabody College of Education & Human Development. His research and teaching interests focus on education policy analysis, causal program evaluation and cost analysis, and the economics of education, with an emphasis on career and technical education, educational accountability policies, and the application of regression discontinuity research designs. Across these substantive areas, he emphasizes how education can address human capital development as well as issues of equity related to race, class, gender, and disability. He is also the proud father of two elementary school-aged children.

Ariana Mangual Figueroa draws from the fields of language socialization and linguistic anthropology to examine language use and learning in Latinx communities living in the United States. Her ethnographic research seeks to understand the ways in which the lives of children and adults in mixed-status families are shaped by citizenship status and schooling practices during everyday, routine interactions. Her work has appeared in *Anthropology & Education Quarterly, Language Policy,* and the *American Educational Research Journal.* She is currently a Coprincipal Investigator of two longitudinal research projects: the first is called the "Putting Immigration and Education into Conversation Everyday" (PIECE) Research Project funded by the W.T. Grant Foundation and the second is the City University of New York-Initiative on Immigration and Education (CUNY-IIE). Prior to obtaining her PhD, she taught English as a Second Language and Spanish in public schools in the Bronx and Brooklyn. She and her husband are currently raising their two daughters in Brooklyn.

Alexandra Freidus is an ethnographer, professor of educational leadership and policy, former social studies teacher, and mom to two young kids. Alex's research and teaching asks what roles educators, policymakers, families, and young people play in sustaining and interrupting racialized patterns in K–12 schools. Through participant-observation, interviews, and public archives, Alex examines how community stakeholders conceptualize student diversity; how school and district administrators enact educational policy; and how these interlocking contexts relate to schools' central work—teaching and learning.

Erin Marie Furtak is Professor of STEM Education and Associate Dean of Faculty in the School of Education at the University of Colorado Boulder. She studies the ways that secondary science teachers design and enact formative assessments, how this process informs teachers' learning and, in turn, how improvements in teachers' formative assessment practice over time relates to student achievement. In particular, she seeks to reframe the design and enactment of classroom and formative assessment in ways that promote more equitable participation in science learning.

Gretchen Givens Generett is Interim Dean and Professor in the School of Education at Duquesne University. She is also the Noble J. Dick Endowed Chair in Community Outreach. Her scholarship intermingles traditional sociology of education, African American studies, and feminist studies with more progressive concepts of justice that examine agency, empowerment, and action. In teaching, Gretchen offers stories as a place for students to recast their individual stories to form a collective narrative that can be used as a catalyst for transformation. She is mother to William, a first-year college student, and Gabrielle, an eighth grader.

Terrance L. Green is an Associate Professor in the Department of Educational Leadership and Policy at the University of Texas. He earned his PhD from the University of Wisconsin-Madison and is a former high school science teacher.

Jacob Hall is an Assistant Professor of Educational Technology in the Childhood/Early Childhood Education Department at SUNY Cortland. His research interests include pre-service teachers' technology integration development, the design of blended courses, and computational thinking in early childhood education. He and his wife live in Syracuse, NY, with their two young sons.

Edmund 'Ted' Hamann is a parent of a 23-year-old (who is out of the house) and a 20-year-old who returned home when his college's switch to remote instruction necessitated it in March 2020. He and his partner Susan raised the kids primarily in Lincoln Nebraska where they all have lived since 2005. But both kids have early memories of living in Providence Rhode Island where the younger one was born and also of the whole family spending a semester abroad in Monterrey Mexico in 2010, when Ted had a visiting professorship at the Universidad de Monterrey and the kids enrolled temporarily in the Instituto Nezaldi, a bilingual private school organized on the principles of the Emilio Reggio with an emphasis on exploratory child-initiated inquiry. In Nebraska both kids graduated from Lincoln High School, the state's second oldest public high school. Ted is a Professor in the Dept. of Teaching, Learning, & Teacher Education at the University of Nebraska-Lincoln, where he has been since 2005. Trained as an anthropologist of education (and current president of the American Anthropology Association's Council on Anthropology and Education), his research has spanned from high school reform, to binational research partnerships, to a biography of pioneering Mexican educator Moisés Sáenz, but his primary area of interest is in studying the local development and contestation of education policy in response to transnational migration and other sources of demographic change. In 2020 he was recognized as an AERA Fellow by the American Educational Research Association and in 2019 spent the fall semester in Tijuana Mexico as a Fulbright García Robles U.S. Scholar.

Decoteau Irby supports groups, collectives, and organizations create conditions for anti-racist organizational learning and continuous improvement with an emphasis on racial equity change. He enjoys playing guitar and recording songs, writing short stories, and designing games and activities that help make a more racially just world. His academic research examines equity-focused school leadership and how it can be used to improve Black children and youth's academic achievement and socioemotional well-being. He is an Associate Professor at University of Illinois at Chicago in the Department of Educational Policy Studies.

Sera J. Hernández is an Assistant Professor in the Dual Language and English Learner Education Department at San Diego State University where she teaches graduate courses on language policy, multilingual education, and biliteracy. She earned her Ph.D. in Education from the University of California, Berkeley and has worked in public pre-K–12 schools and universities across California for over 20 years. With an interdisciplinary academic background, her research bridges the fields of educational linguistics and the anthropology of education to examine the sociocultural, linguistic, and political contexts surrounding educational language policies, bilingual teacher preparation, and bilingualism and biliteracy practices, particularly in border regions around the world. She is currently investigating the professional development experiences of binational educators working and living near the Mexico-U.S. border. Her scholarship has been featured in the *Review of Research in Education*, the *CATESOL Journal*, *Journal of Latinos and Education*, *Children's Literature in Education*, and several edited volumes. She enjoys spending quality time with her 11-year-old daughter Savannah and her 8-year-old son Samuel.

Bong Gee Jang is an Assistant Professor in the Department of Reading and Language Arts at Syracuse University. His main areas of research include literacy motivation, engagement in digital settings, and disciplinary/ content literacy. His research has appeared in such journals as *Reading Research Quarterly*, *Journal of Literacy Research*, *Educational Psychology Review*, *Literacy Research: Theory, Method, and Practice*, *Journal of Adolescent & Adult Literacy*, and *The Reading Teacher*. Bong Gee teaches courses related to disciplinary literacy and language arts for both preservice and in-service teachers. He also teaches introductory and advanced research methods courses to graduate students.

Jing Lei is a Professor and Department Chair in Instructional Design, Development and Evaluation in the School of Education at Syracuse University. Dr. Lei's scholarship focuses on the integration of technology in educational settings, eLearning, social-cultural and psychological impact of technology, teacher technology preparation, and emerging technologies for education. She teaches courses and advises students at undergraduate, master's and doctoral levels.

Rebecca Lowenhaupt is an Associate Professor of Educational Leadership in the Lynch School of Education at Boston College. A former middle-school teacher and current parent of two middle-schoolers, she teaches aspiring school and district leaders about teacher supervision, organizational theory, and research methods. Drawing on multiple methods of empirical research, her research investigates educational leadership and policy in the context of immigration with a focus on new immigrant destinations. Funded by the W.T. Grant Foundation, her current project supports a research-practice partnership with six school districts around the country to share and design practices to support immigrant-origin students. Her scholarship has appeared in several academic journals, including the *American Education Research Journal, Leadership and Policy in Schools,* and the *Journal of Educational Administration*. During the pandemic, her children have become painters, cartoonists, woodworkers, and chefs.

Joanne M. Marshall is a former high school teacher and a current associate professor in the School of Education at Iowa State University, where she teaches in the teacher preparation program. She researches religion and social justice pedagogy in the context of preparation programs. She holds a doctorate from the Harvard University Graduate School of Education and is the lead editor for the work-life balance book series of Information Age Publishing. She is the parent of two teens, who, as a result of pandemic growth spurts, are much taller than she and now refer to her as "Fun-Sized," as if she is a Halloween candy bar.

Melissa A. Martinez is a native of Brownsville, Texas and is a former bilingual school teacher and counselor. She is currently an associate professor in the Educational and Community Leadership master's and PhD in School Improvement programs at Texas State University. In this role, she is passionate about preparing and supporting school and district leaders who are critical practitioner scholars that can meet the needs of culturally and linguistically diverse communities. This commitment is reflected in her research, which focuses on three primary strands pertaining to equity and access along the P–20 education continuum: (1) college access, college readiness, and college-going cultures for underserved communities, (2) social justice and equity-oriented leadership preparation and Latinx leadership/leaders, and (3) the experiences of faculty of color in academia. Dr. Martinez's scholarship can be found in various outlets including *Teachers College Record, Educational Administration Quarterly, Race Ethnicity and Educa-*

tion, and *Urban Review.* She is also coeditor of two books: *Latino educational leadership: Serving Latino communities and preparing Latinx leaders across the P–20 pipeline* and *Latinas Leading Schools.* She loves cooking plant-based meals and enjoys spending time with her family, gardening, traveling, and yoga.

Raquel Muñiz is an attorney and an Assistant Professor of law and education policy at the Lynch School of Education and Human Development at Boston College, as well as a liaison with the College of Law. As a sociolegal scholar, her research agenda includes two lines of inquiry: (1) examining the role of the law and accompanying policies in furthering educational equity for all students, particularly students who have experienced substantial adversity throughout their lives; and (2) examining the use of research evidence in the legal system and public policy decision-making where such decision-making has implications for educational equity.

Gabrielle Oliveira is an assistant professor at the Lynch School of Education and Human Development at Boston College. She was born and raised in São Paulo, Brazil, and is an anthropologist of education. Her work with immigrant populations in and out of the United States has spanned more than a decade. She received her master as well as doctorate degrees from Columbia University and Teachers College. Gabrielle is the author of *Motherhood Across Borders: Immigrants and their Children in Mexico and New York,* published by NYU Press.

Mario Rios Perez specializes in the history of migration, race, and education at Syracuse University where he is an Associate Professor in the Department of Cultural Foundations of Education and faculty affiliate in Women's and Gender Studies. He is author of the forthcoming book titled *Subjects of Resistance: Education, Race, and Transnational Life in Mexican Chicago, 1910–1940* (Rutgers University Press).

Patrick Proctor is a Professor in the Lynch School of Education and Human Development at Boston College. He studies language use and development in multilingual classrooms. His broader expertise ranges from bilingualism and second language acquisition to curriculum development and language policy in U.S. schools.

Sharon Radd is an Associate Professor and Program Director of Organizational Leadership at St. Catherine University in St. Paul, MN, an Equity Fellow at the Midwest, and Plains Equity Assistance Center at IUPUI, and the Founder of ConsciousPraxis. Her research and practice in the field center on leadership development that is critically-grounded, equity-focused, human-centered, and systems-based. Her work advances the theoretical, conceptual, and empirical understanding of adult learning, organizational change, discursive functioning, and public engagement of individuals, groups, organizations, and societies.

Jessica Rigby is an Associate Professor in the College of Education at the University of Washington. She uses lenses from organizational sociology to understand the role of school and district leaders in the implementation of policy, classroom instruction, and improving teacher practice towards increasing equitable learning opportunities for historically marginalized communities. Her current work is in partnership with a team of school and district leaders in a local district, codesigning and implementing inquiry cycles to try out leadership practices towards anti-racist, ambitious mathematics instruction. When she's not sitting in front of her computer, you might catch her running to catch up with her toddler and pup in the parks and mountains of the Pacific Northwest.

Rosa L. Rivera-McCutchen is an Associate Professor & Coordinator of Building & District Leader graduate programs at Lehman College CUNY, and an affiliated doctoral faculty member in the Urban Education PhD Program at CUNY Graduate Center. Dr. Rivera-McCutchen began her career as a high school teacher in the Bronx before earning her doctorate at NYU. A first-generation college graduate, her research is informed by her experiences attending and teaching in NYC public schools. Dr. Rivera-McCutchen's work focuses on urban school leaders who practice "radical care," which centers anti-racism and equity as part of their leadership work. Her research has appeared in *Educational Administration Quarterly, Urban Education, Journal of School Leadership, Journal of Cases in Educational Leadership,* among other journals. Dr. Rivera-McCutchen's forthcoming book is entitled *Radical Care: Leading for Justice in Urban Schools* (Teachers College Press).

Dalia Rodriguez is Associate Professor of Cultural Foundations of Education and associated faculty in Women's and Gender Studies at Syracuse University. Her main interests include race, ethnicity, and gender in education. Her teaching and research interests examine women of color feminisms and qualitative research methods. She has a special interest in testimonial writing. Her scholarship includes centering women of color in the academy, undergraduate and graduates. She focuses on stories about how students resist and navigate white supremacy and patriarchy, and what this means for the liberation of women of color in various higher educational contexts, including college classrooms. She has also written extensively about the silencing and erasure of women of color, and how to disrupt mechanisms of silence.

Noreen Naseem Rodríguez is an Assistant Professor in the School of Education at Iowa State University. She is an interdisciplinary scholar who uses critical race frameworks to explore Asian American educational experiences, diverse children's literature, and the teaching of difficult histories to young people. She received the 2019 Early Career Award from the Children's Literature Assembly of the National Council of Teachers of English and the 2017 Larry Metcalf Exemplary Dissertation Award from the National Council of the Social Studies. Her work has been published in *Curriculum Inquiry, Theory & Research in Social Education, The International Journal of Multicultural Education, The Social Studies,* and *School Library Journal.* She is the author of the forthcoming book *Social Studies For A Better World: An Anti-Oppressive Approach for Elementary Educators* with Katy Swalwell (W.W. Norton) and was a bilingual elementary educator in Texas for nine years.

Diego Román is an Assistant Professor in Bilingual/Bicultural Education at the Department of Curriculum and Instruction at the University of Wisconsin-Madison. Dr. Román's research interests are located at the intersection of applied linguistics, bilingual education, and science education. Specifically, he investigates the implicit and explicit ideologies reflected in the design and implementation of bilingual and science education programs particularly on how environmental topics are taught to multilingual students. He conducts his research from a Systemic Functional Linguistics perspective by analyzing the linguistic and multimodal characteristics of the discourse that take place in bilingual and science classrooms. Dr. Román has researched the language used to teach climate change at the middle school level and is currently examining science, environmental, and bilingual programs (Spanish/English and Kichwa/Spanish) in rural Wisconsin and in Ecuador. He is a 2020 Spencer Foundation/National Academy of Education Postdoctoral fellow.

Carrie Sampson is an assistant professor in the Division of Educational Leadership and Innovation at Mary Lou Fulton Teachers College, Arizona State University. She has a Ph.D. in Public Affairs, M.S. in Cultural Foundations of Education, graduate certificate in Women's Studies, and a BS in Economics. Her research focuses largely on district and state level policymaking, school boards, school desegregation, and community advocacy in education.

Carolyn Sattin-Bajaj is an Associate Professor in the Department of Education in the Gevirtz Graduate School of Education at the University of California, Santa Barbara, and mom to two elementary school-aged boys. Her research focuses on issues of educational access and equity for immigrant-origin youth and other historically underserved student populations. Her work includes exploratory qualitative studies of immigrant and homeless families' school choice behaviors; experimental research to develop and test interventions to reduce educational inequities; studies of school leaders' responses to xenophobia in schools and society and their preparedness to address the consequences of immigration enforcement and racism for their school communities; and research on the ways that teacher education programs prepare preservice teachers to educate children in immigrant families. Carolyn is author of *Unaccompanied Minors: Immigrant Youth, School Choice, and the Pursuit of Equity* (Harvard Education Press, 2014).

Martin Scanlan is an Associate Professor in the Department of Educational Leadership and Higher Education in the Lynch School of Education and Human Development at Boston College. From 2006–2013 he was a faculty member in the College of Education at Marquette University. Before becoming a faculty in higher education, Scanlan spent a decade working in teaching and administration in urban elementary and middle schools in Washington, D.C., Berkeley, CA, and Madison, WI. In his doctoral work in Educational Leadership and Policy Analysis at the University of Wisconsin–Madison he studied the intersectionality of inclusivity in urban elementary schools serving traditionally marginalized students. Since 2005 he has worked in institutes of higher education as a teacher and scholar. His scholarship examines systemic transformation of school systems toward integrated service delivery and on asset-oriented approaches to educating culturally and linguistically diverse students. In particular, he supports communities of practice helping adults advance toward these ends, and he continues to work closely with building- and district-level administrators to bridge research and practice. His most recent works include two co-edited volumes: *Leadership for Culturally and Linguistically Responsive Education: Designing Networks That Transform Schools*, published in 2019 by Harvard Education Press, and *Leadership for Increasingly Diverse Schools*, published in 2020 by Routledge.

Rachel Silver is an Assistant Professor of Education at York University and Codirector of the Borderless Higher Education for Refugees (BHER) Project. Her research explores how discourses, programs, and policies on gender in international development education intersect with young people's lives. Rachel has conducted extensive ethnographic fieldwork in

Southeastern Africa and in the United States. She lives in Toronto with her partner, two children, and dog.

Kate Spence is an associate professor in the Sammartino School of Education at Fairleigh Dickinson University. She is the director of the QUEST program, through which students can obtain a BA in the liberal arts and sciences along with an MA in teaching in five years. Kate's experiences as a 7–12 English Language Arts teacher and professional development coach in a range of settings, including rural VT, suburban MD, and urban NYC, have led to a commitment to equitable public education for all students. Her work with pre-service and practicing teachers is focused on preparing and supporting educators in creating inclusive, equitable K–12 learning environments and learning experiences for all students. She is mom to two energetic, elementary school-aged boys and can be reached at kspence@fdu.edu.

Corrie Stone-Johnson is Associate Professor of Educational Administration at the University at Buffalo, SUNY. Her research examines the social and cultural aspects of change and school leadership, highlighting how people interact to foster or impede reform in a context of accountability. Her work has been published in journals including *Educational Administration Quarterly, Education and Urban Society,* and *Teachers and Teaching: Theory and Practice*. In 2016 she published the book *Generational Identity, Educational Change, and School Leadership* with Routledge. She is the Editor-in-Chief of the *Journal of Educational Change* and is on the advisory board of *Leadership and Policy in Schools*. Corrie lives in Buffalo, New York with her husband (brilliant chocolatier), daughter (aspiring elite rower), son (budding tech guru), and dog (main talent is napping).

Katharine O. Strunk is a Professor of education policy and, by courtesy, economics, and the Clifford E. Erickson Distinguished Chair in Education at Michigan State University. She is also the faculty director of the Michigan State University Education Policy Innovation Collaborative (EPIC) and president of the Association for Education Finance and Policy (AEFP). Katharine's current research through EPIC is focused on working with local and state education agencies on studies that will help them inform policy and practice. Rooted in the fields of economics and public policy, Katharine's work centers on structures that are central to district operations and policy and the ways these structures affect policymakers' decisions and outcomes. Katharine is mom to two wonderful and active twin boys, dog-mom to a pandemic puppy, and married to a fantastic partner. They all live in (semi-)controlled chaos in East Lansing, Michigan.

George Theoharis is a Professor of Teaching and Leadership at Syracuse University. He has experience as a school principal and teacher; at SU he served as Department Chair, Associate Dean for Urban Partnerships, and Director of Field Relations. His work preparing leaders and teachers as well as partnering with schools focuses on issues of equity, justice, diversity, inclusion, and school reform. George's work bridges the worlds of K–12 schools and higher education. He writes for public audiences in: *The School Administrator, The Washington Post, The Root,* and *The Syracuse Post-Standard* as well in many books and scholarly articles. His most recent books are *Five Practices for Equity Focused School Leadership* (2021) and *Leadership for Increasingly Diverse Schools* (2020). George grew up in Wisconsin in an activist family committed to making a more just world. Cooking and feeding people are his favorite hobbies. He lives in Fayetteville, NY with his two awesome children and his father.

Erica O. Turner is an Associate Professor of education policy at the University of Wisconsin–Madison. Her research examines racism and inequity—and efforts to challenge those—in education policy and practice. Through her research and teaching she seeks to deepen how we conceptualize policy problems, racial equity, educational aims, and policy alternatives and ultimately to contribute to the knowledge necessary to make public schooling more equitable and just. Her book *Suddenly Diverse: How School Districts Manage Race and Inequality* (University of Chicago Press, 2020) examines how school district leaders' in two Midwestern school districts who respond to demographic change and growing inequality in their schools with equity discourses and business-inspired policy tools that perpetuate existing inequalities and advance new forms of racism. She is a former middle school teacher and a current parent to three children, ages 11 months, 7 years, and 10 years.

Jennie Weiner is an Associate Professor of educational leadership at UConn. She is committed to use her research and voice to shift our definition and enactment of educational leadership to make it more inclusive and equity oriented. This includes engaging in research focused on gender discrimination and gendered racism in educational leadership. She also focuses on leadership and organizational change particularly in chronically under-performing and under-resourced schools and districts. Her book, coauthored with Dr. Isobel Stevenson, *The Strategy Playbook for Educational Leaders: Principles and Processes* (Routledge, 2020), is a practical guide for educational leaders to support planning grounded in equity, coherence, capacity-building, and logic. Along with her partner, she is currently juggling her teaching and research with the virtual schooling of 9-year-old twin boys who have been home since March 13, 2020 and looks forward to having some semblance of her life and brain back in the future.

Susan W. Woolley is Associate Professor of Educational Studies and LGBTQ Studies and the Director of the LGBTQ Studies Program at Colgate University. Her research focuses on gender and sexuality in schools and the educational experiences of LGBTQ youth. Her scholarship has appeared in *Gender and Education, TSQ: Transgender Studies Quarterly, Journal of Bisexuality, Intersections: Critical Issues in Education, International Journal for the Sociology of Language, Journal of Language and Sexuality,* and *Anthropology & Education Quarterly.* Her recent book coedited with Lee Airton, *Teaching about Gender Diversity: Teacher-Tested Lesson Plans for K–12 classrooms,* was published by Canadian Scholars Press in 2020. Susan Woolley has been honored as a Concha Delgado Gaitan Presidential Fellow by the Council on Anthropology and Education for her work.

Sarah Woulfin is an Associate Professor of educational leadership at the University of Connecticut. She uses organizational theory and qualitative methods to study the relationship between policy, leadership, and equitable learning opportunities. She has conducted multiple studies on instructional coaching. Dr. Woulfin is a coeditor of *Educational Researcher.* Prior to her doctoral studies at the University of California, Berkeley, Sarah was an elementary school teacher and reading coach from 2000–2006. Sarah enjoys running, drinking coffee, and researching Minecraft with her child.

4/5/23

CPSIA information can be obtained
at www.ICGtesting.com
Printed in the USA
LVHW041635200223
739952LV00004B/206